"Never underestimate the power of small talk! This brilliant book demonstrates how ordinary conversations about weather can create extraordinary opportunities for reconfiguring human relationships with nature and the living world. If you are curious about how we can radically reframe our responses to the environmental crisis through education and beyond, this book is for you."

Professor Iveta Silova, *Associate Dean of Global Engagement at Mary Lou Fulton Teachers College, Arizona State University*

"Rooney and Blaise invite us into a lively world of child-weather encounters and offer an important new paradigm for environmental education. This book shows us how learning with children with weather can embrace humility, surprise, and delight, without turning away from troubling uncertainties of a climate changing world."

Associate Professor Astrida Neimanis, *Canada Research Chair in Feminist Environmental Humanities, UBC Okanagan*

"Pause, attend, attune, notice – these are the invitations that this extraordinary book offers to readers. Meticulous tracings are presented of weather learning through modalities of doing, walking, writing, making and becoming. Environmental education opens to complexity, vulnerability, and responsibility as we humans come to understand that we are inherently entangled in volatile ecologies and constantly shifting relations with and in the world. This book shows how this urgent work must start in early childhood education. Children's intimate encounters with weather extend from everyday moments in open spaces and playgrounds to deep time, Indigenous time, colonial time and the ever-present times of human-induced climate change. The authors introduce practices for how we might envisage and work towards new weather worlds and make a significant and fresh contribution to posthuman educational research."

Professor Suzanne Gannon, *University of Western Sydney*

"In rethinking climate change as something 'already part of children's lives,' this beautiful book offers an alternative mode for engaging with precarious futures and troubled presents. Whilst grappling with big questions, the authors ground us in small moments and micro sensations of how children and adults experience time, place and climate; as dust in nostrils or rain chilling the surface of the skin, for example. It gently guides us away from the certainty and solutions we are often told are required, inviting us instead to reimagine how we might respond to, learn with or listen to a changing climate. This is a poignant yet hopeful book, where hope is offered outside of a framing of mastery or certainty, through a commitment to ongoing-ness and the understanding that 'many worlds are possible.'"

Dr Abigail Hackett, *Reader, Manchester Metropolitan University*

"As I read outdoors, the wind strokes my cheek along with the sound of bumblebees buzzing in the sunshine. This book makes you pay attention and participate with weather worlds and contributes to an understanding of how we are inter-connected with other worlds, humans and non-humans. By bringing the weather to the fore, the book invites us to consider planetary well-being and care. In an inquiring and inspiring way, the authors offer an alternative way of thinking, learning, and practicing with all encounters in the field of early childhood and environmental learning. This is a book we cannot do without."

Associate Professor Anne Myrstad, *UIT – The Arctic University of Norway*

"This transformative book brings climate home via everyday weather, cultivating wisdom for new action-relations. Rooney and Blaise elegantly dissolve borders around 'the environment,' learning and showing relations already in place, which children already know. Rather than seeing 'the environment' as a distinct, separate entity, intentionally renewing weather awareness reveals our place within a living, breathing, participative community of more-than-human beings."

Associate Professor Sandra Wooltorton, *Nulungu Research Institute, University of Notre Dame Australia*

RETHINKING ENVIRONMENTAL EDUCATION IN A CLIMATE CHANGE ERA

As the impact of climate change has become harder to ignore, it has become increasingly evident that children will inherit futures where climate challenges require new ways of thinking about how humans can live better with the world. This book re-situates weather in early childhood education, examining people as inherently a part of and affected by nature, and challenges the positioning of humans at the centre of progress and decision-making.

Exploring the ways children can learn with weather, this book for researchers and advanced students, works with the pedagogical potential in children's relations with weather as a vital way of connecting with and responding to wider climate concerns.

Tonya Rooney is a Senior Lecturer in Early Childhood and Environmental Education at the Australian Catholic University. She is member of the Common Worlds Research Collective.

Mindy Blaise is a Vice Chancellor's Professorial Research Fellow and Co-Director of the Centre for People, Place, and Planet, at Edith Cowan University, Western Australia. She is a co-founder of the Common Worlds Research Collective and #FEAS Feminist Educators Against Sexism.

Contesting Early Childhood
Series Editors: Liselott Mariett Olsson
and Michel Vandenbroeck

This ground-breaking series questions the current dominant discourses surrounding early childhood, and offers instead alternative narratives of an area that is now made up of a multitude of perspectives and debates.

The series examines the possibilities and risks arising from the accelerated development of early childhood services and policies, and illustrates how it has become increasingly steeped in regulation and control. Insightfully, this collection of books shows how early childhood services can in fact contribute to ethical and democratic practices. The authors explore new ideas taken from alternative working practices in both the western and developing world, and from other academic disciplines such as developmental psychology. Current theories and best practice are placed in relation to the major processes of political, social, economic, cultural and technological change occurring in the world today.

Revisiting Paulo Freire's Pedagogy of the Oppressed
Issues and Challenges in Early Childhood Education
Edited by Michel Vandenbroeck

Neoliberalism and Early Childhood Education
Markets, Imaginaries and Governance
Guy Roberts-Holmes and Peter Moss

In Dialogue with Reggio Emilia
Listening, researching and learning (2e)
Carlina Rinaldi

Rethinking Environmental Education in a Climate Change Era
Weather Learning in Early Childhood
Tonya Rooney and Mindy Blaise

Slow Knowledge and the Unhurried Child
Time for Slow Pedagogies in Early Childhood Education
Alison Clark

For more information about this series, please visit: www.routledge.com/
Contesting-Early-Childhood/book-series/SE0623

RETHINKING ENVIRONMENTAL EDUCATION IN A CLIMATE CHANGE ERA

Weather Learning in Early Childhood

Tonya Rooney and Mindy Blaise

LONDON AND NEW YORK

Designed cover image: © Vicki Jauron, Babylon and Beyond Photography/Getty Images

First published 2023
by Routledge
4 Park Square, Milton Park, Abingdon, Oxon OX14 4RN

and by Routledge
605 Third Avenue, New York, NY 10158

Routledge is an imprint of the Taylor & Francis Group, an informa business

© 2023 Tonya Rooney and Mindy Blaise

The right of Tonya Rooney and Mindy Blaise to be identified as authors of this work has been asserted in accordance with sections 77 and 78 of the Copyright, Designs and Patents Act 1988.

All rights reserved. No part of this book may be reprinted or reproduced or utilised in any form or by any electronic, mechanical, or other means, now known or hereafter invented, including photocopying and recording, or in any information storage or retrieval system, without permission in writing from the publishers.

Trademark notice: Product or corporate names may be trademarks or registered trademarks, and are used only for identification and explanation without intent to infringe.

British Library Cataloguing-in-Publication Data
A catalogue record for this book is available from the British Library

ISBN: 978-0-367-71344-7 (hbk)
ISBN: 978-0-367-71346-1 (pbk)
ISBN: 978-1-003-15041-1 (ebk)

DOI: 10.4324/9781003150411

Typeset in Bembo
by KnowledgeWorks Global Ltd.

CONTENTS

List of Figures	*ix*
Series Editors' Foreword	*x*
Acknowledgements	*xiii*

PART I
A Weather Learning Project   **1**

1   Introduction   3

2   Young Children and Environmental Education   15

PART II
Methods: Thinking, Moving and Writing with Weather   **31**

3   Thinking with Weather   33

4   Walking with Weather   49

5   Writing Small Weather Stories   63

PART III
Relations: Weathering with More-Than-Human Worlds   **79**

6   Bodies, Atmospheres and Affects   81

viii Contents

7 Multi-Species Weather Encounters 94

8 Earth and Deep Weather Times 112

PART IV
Responses: Learning and Speculating in a Climate Change Era **127**

9 Weather Learning 129

10 Conclusion: An Invitation to Weather Together 143

Index *149*

FIGURES

3.1	Walking with shadows	36
3.2	Falling bark shelter	38
3.3	*Ngaraka: Shrine for the lost Koori* with rain and child	43
3.4	"Hold on to your hat"	45
4.1	Walking place	50
4.2	Limestone "claw" marks	51
4.3	Wild urban lakeside	52
4.4	Weather surfaces	57
5.1	Muddy puddles	72
6.1	"There's a sun in my tummy"	82
6.2	Dead fish conversations	88
7.1	Eastern Water Dragon encounter	99
7.2	Reaching out to a possum tail	101
7.3	Gathering feathers	103
7.4	Making smoke	106
7.5	Marks of rain and fire	107
8.1	Everything is moving. Always	113
8.2	Making a dust storm	115
9.1	"We are already here"	130
9.2	Making rain	139

SERIES EDITORS' FOREWORD

Liselott Mariett Olsson and Michel Vandenbroeck

One would think that there is only so much to say about weather in education. This book, however, shows that there is an abundance of things to say and things to do on the topic in educational practice and theory, not the least in the early years. Not only is the topic treated in all its potential richness by authors Tonya Rooney and Mindy Blaise but they also situate it in relation to what may be considered one of the most important societal and educational questions of our time: the human being's time and place in nature.

The book and its beautiful stories are not only dealing with such an existential-environmental question in a rich way; the book is also situated in very rich environments: a close collaboration with children and early childhood educators gives a multitude of wonderful empirical examples of children's relations with weather; and theoretical collaborations with resources from Indigenous, feminist, new materialist, post-humanist and post-developmental perspectives as well as perspectives from the fields of childhood studies, children's geographies and environmental education deepen the understanding we may have of both learning and of weather. Together these practical and theoretical resources function in what comes forward as an "ecology of action and thought" that both widens and intensifies the question of the human being's time and place in nature as it may be understood within early childhood education and care.

If early childhood education and care, and education tout court, in some original sense is about creating time and space for the new generation to study and transform culture, knowledge and values, then this book gives us ample examples of what that may look like in relation to the here chosen existential-environmental question. But if education also in some sense is about listening to children, then this book shows that children have a very profound relation to nature that also adults may learn from. If children "give life" to more-than-human

Series editors' foreword **xi**

matters and things (something which there are ample and wonderful examples of in the book), this may not necessarily be considered as a sign of lack in rational thinking. As the book shows, it may rather be considered a more profound relation and act of care that, had adults adopted and adapted to this, we might have been elsewhere than in the profound climate-crisis where we find ourselves today. And yet, such insights into children's relations with weather and other natural phenomena are here not reducing the question to concern only the child per se, but rather the relation between human and nature itself. In that sense, the book is avoiding any "all too human" approach as well as "throwing out the baby with the bathwater" and rather frames the question in a profound relational educational way: to have rich opportunities to have one's deep multi-sensuous and symbolic relations with nature nurtured at an early age may also imply being able to deeply care for the common and natural world.

The book clearly shows in practice and theory what this could look like. It does not avoid the complex issue of bringing the current climate-crisis, created by adults and to be inherited by the new generation, into the context of childhood and education in the early years. Importantly, though, and as the authors state early in the book: it is here not a question of positioning children either in terms of our only future hope or within hopeless despair. It is rather a question of evoking the deeply relational, even intertwined, aspects of human and nature already there that give this book its direction in suggesting important alternatives to environmental education in the early years. In that sense the authors' insistence upon learning with weather rather than about weather must be considered an important deal-breaker. In fact, education when aiming for children and students to learn about something, by necessity introduces a distance between that which is studied and those who study it. Here, however, the intimate relation between human and nature is given precedence; the relation comes, in time and space, before the individual human intellect, and it is that deep metaphysical relationality that make children and adults alike learn with weather in the present book.

In that sense too, the book challenges accounts of education built upon intellectual certainties and transmission of facts from one that knows to one that does not know – to learn with weather eludes contemporary rigidities forced upon education through a historically oblivious and future-obsessed abstract reduction of the aims and means of education. Instead, the book seems to share the old-age, yet perhaps more relevant than ever, argument of French philosopher Henri Bergson (1859–1941) that claimed that a theory of knowledge must not be entirely separated from a theory of the biological evolution of life; as the biological evolution of life on the planet is what both generates and transgresses the human intellect there is a need for both critical and creative methodologies capable of aligning themselves with the long evolutionary time where human and world endure, dure and decay in concert (Bergson, 2007/1907). The present book seems affined to this as it tells the story of how environmental education in an era of climate-change and learning with weather, may, methodologically

xii Series editors' foreword

and creatively, take stock of the past while intensively exploring the present with attention tuned to unknown futures to come.

Perhaps such a critical-creative and "timely" approach is precisely what is needed not only in education and the early years, but also in other social and political attempts to question our existential-environmental presence on the planet today. If so, this book not only stays close to this book-series' attempts to widen the aesthetical, ethical and political questions posed within the early years, but also breaks the ground for new practices and new understandings of the human being's place and time in nature that exceed and appeal to fields beyond early childhood education and care.

Reference

Bergson, H. (1907/2007). *Creative evolution*. Palgrave Macmillan.

ACKNOWLEDGEMENTS

There are several places, funding bodies, events, people and some of our approaches to the writing of this book that we want to acknowledge. We see our acknowledgements as part of our feminist citational practices because they help us to be transparent about how we work, who we are thinking with, and the multiple ways that we have been supported financially, intellectually and personally. First, we want to acknowledge that the walking research this book is based on took place on Ngunnawal and Ngambri Country. We have also written parts of this book on the lands of the Wiradjuri people, of the Walbanja people of the Yuin Nation, and Whadjuk Noongar boodja. These lands have never been ceded, and we pay our respects to the First Nation custodians of this Country and its land, air and waterways. We acknowledge that we are situated as non-Indigenous people in a place that has been invaded and colonised. We have chosen not to use the term settler to place ourselves, as our presence seems so much more implicated than the act of settling. We acknowledge that using the term non-Indigenous is also far from perfect in conveying the tensions entangled in our presence in Australia and that Indigenous people may have language more adequate to this task.

We also want to acknowledge that we do not come to researching weather–child relations and weather learning from nowhere. We both come from *somewhere* and this matters. For instance, Tonya spent much of her childhood in regional NSW on the Western slopes of the Great Dividing Range. She remembers dry hot summers punctuated by storms, bushfires and long periods of drought. A favourite hangout for the local kids was a creek brimming with yabbies and tadpoles. The shape of the land – granite outcrops, hills, grassy plains and wandering creeks – stayed with her and surfaces as deep and familiar when she encounters similar landscapes. Mindy migrated to Australia over 20 years ago and has lived for most of that time in Melbourne, Victoria. Perth

xiv Acknowledgements

and Western Australia are new places to her. She was born in Baton Rouge, Louisiana, and the Mississippi River grew her up. She remembers hot muggy summers walking along Bayou Goula as a child, with dragon flies buzzing while picking pecans with her grandmother. Now, while walking with and listening to bilya stories, those southern Louisiana atmospheres are always lingering with her.

We think it is necessary and important to note that climate change and the pandemic have disrupted everyone's lives, including our plans to collaboratively write together. With a little bit of hope and naivety, we thought that things would return to normal; that we wouldn't need to worry about forests disappearing because of bushfires, that Mindy could leave and get back into the fortress known as Western Australia; that we wouldn't feel so fatigued from worrying about family and friends keeping safe and healthy. This "new normal" meant that we had to come up with different ways of collaborating and writing together. This was primarily done over Zoom and involved weekly book meetings, blocking out our calendars for uninterrupted writing time, scheduling time for shorter and intense writing that we would then follow with talking. We would be lying if we said this way of working was fine. We miss the in-person walking, talking and writing together. Working on this project during this period helped us understand that we will need to continue to be creative in finding ways to work and live differently.

In multiple ways this work has been supported financially, intellectually and emotionally by various organisations, people and more-than-human worlds. The project has been financially supported by a Partnership Development Grant from the Social Sciences and Humanities Research Council, Canada, led by Veronica Pacini-Ketchabaw. The name of the project was *The Climate Action Network: Exploring Climate Change Pedagogies with Children* and this project created the Weather Collaboratory. This funding allowed us to bring Felicity Royds into our team as a research assistant. Some of our initial musings with feminist environmental humanities, young children and weather were activated in the project, *The Wild Weathering Collaboratory: Reaclimatising Early Childhood Environmental Pedagogies to the Prospects of Anthropogenic Climate Change,* supported by the Seedbox Collaboratory, funded by mistra (Swedish Foundation for Strategic Environmental Research) and formas (The Swedish Research Council for the Environmental, Agricultural Sciences and Spatial Planning).

Tonya would like to acknowledge financial support from the Australian Catholic University's (ACU) Research Study Program that enabled time away from teaching duties and made this work possible. Mindy would like to acknowledge the financial support of the Edith Cowan University Vice Chancellor's Professorial Fellowship. This funded her and Jo Pollitt's participation in the project. Both of our universities have supported us to travel and present at educational research conferences such as the American Educational Research Association and the Australian Association for Research in Education, where we were able to share initial findings and emerging ideas about weather learning.

Acknowledgements **xv**

The University Preschool and Child Care Centre (UPCCC) preschool provided time for staff to participate on our regular walks from 2016 to 2019. We thank the director, Helen Chan, for her ongoing support; previous director, Lynley Rees, who welcomed us from the beginning; the educators, including Jessie, Veena, Tongbo, Paula, Bingo and others; the children's families; and the children, whose words and wonderings we draw on throughout this book.

It is important that we make it known loud and clear that our thinking and scholarship is never done alone. As well as acknowledging key theorists, practices, places and networks that inform our thinking throughout the book, we are also part of several feminist research collectives, such as the Common Worlds Research Collective, The Ediths and #FEAS, Feminist Educators Against Sexism. In addition, the Centre for People, Place, & Planet and the School of Education, at Edith Cowan University has also been an intellectually inviting place to share our work.

We both have so many people to thank for their support, in a myriad of ways. Tonya would like to thank Mindy for her generous scholarship and for always pushing our thinking and practice that bit further. The book is better for this. Tonya has valued the creative experimentation that was possible in our walking, talking and thinking together. This work started in 2016 as a collaboration with Affrica Taylor on the project *Walking with Wildlife in Wild Weather Times*. Tonya is grateful to have Affrica as mentor, colleague and friend, and small threads from many of their conversations have found their way into this book. Veronica Pacini-Ketchabaw brought together an amazing international community in the *Climate Action Network* that allowed this work to continue, and Jo Pollit and Felicity Royds brought fresh and important insights to the project. Over the past few years, Tonya's writing companions Judith Norris and Kathrine Whitty provided much-needed encouragement that kept the project moving. Tonya's research was also made possible with the support of Carolyn Broadbent and colleagues in the ACU School of Education, as well as research leaders in the ACU Institute for Learning Sciences and Teacher Education, Joce Nuttall and Suzy Edwards. Scholars from other universities including Iris Duhn, Cassandra Phoenix and Sarah Hennessy engaged in important conversations on ideas of walking, learning and weather. Tonya also thanks the online Master of Teaching (Early Childhood and Primary) students at ACU for lively class conversations and their passion to think differently about the future of education.

For Mindy, working with Tonya over the years has been stimulating, generative and insightful. She has loved walking, talking, thinking, writing and weathering together with Tonya and has learned how to be a more attuned scholar through this collaboration. Mindy's work colleagues Jo Pollitt, Jane Merewether, Pierre Horwitz, Lyndall Adams, Wendy Bartuccio, Lennie Barblett, Caroline Finch, Stefania Giamminuti, Naomi Godden, Madlen Griffiths, Angela Hill, Libby Jackson-Barrett, Nicola Johnson, Sophia Nimphius, Maggie McAlinden, Cindy McClean, Dawn Penney, Zack Weedon, and the cohort of postgraduates Ali Blackwell, Emma Fishwick, Karen Nociti, Claire O'Callaghan, Katie Pritchard,

xvi Acknowledgements

Vanessa Wintoneak and Kylie Wrigley at Edith Cowan University have all contributed to an enriching and supportive work environment. Mindy would like to acknowledge the significant impact that feminist artist-scholar Jo Pollitt has had on her work. Jo's choreographic sensibilities and generous ways of collaborating have shaped and influenced Mindy's weather learning. In addition, Lilly Blue and the Art Gallery of Western Australia have supported and informed some of the initial creative and collaborative weather thinking that has seeped into weather learning. Mindy is fortunate to also have a diverse and broad network of scholar friends who keep her going; thank you Veronica Pacini-Ketchabaw, Affrica Taylor, Iveta Silova, Emily Gray, Jacqueline Ullman, Lucy Nichols, Deana Leahy, Sue Grieshaber, Sharon Ryan, Catherine Hamm, Sandra Wooltorton, Hillevi Lenz Taguchi, Sarah Truman and so many more.

Since 2015 we have participated in several Bush Salons held in Wee Jasper, NSW. These were often with Affrica Taylor, Lesley Instone, Astrida Neimanis, Jo Pollitt, Catherine Hamm, Veronica Pacini-Ketchabaw and colleagues, to generate feminist, collaborative, creative and inclusive methods and practices in collaboration with the valley and its more-than-human inhabitants. The Bush Salons provided regular points of reckoning for our work, as we were continually invited by creek and mountain to reflect on the more-than-human collaboration that emerges in the practice of writing and the doing of creative work such as painting, weaving or writing.

There is little doubt that academic work is often felt across our personal lives. Tonya would like to thank her family and friends who have supported her writing journey. For the bush walks, the river swims, the camping expeditions, dusty road trips, beach combing, mountain walks and for hanging out at home in lockdown times, Tonya is indebted to Lea Durie and to Tilda, Rory and Jess. This and other life adventures would not be the same without you.

Mindy simply cannot write this acknowledgement without giving a shout out to the "Dog Park Ladies" and their canine companions who were her and Lobito's lifeline during the pandemic, when she and Lo was literally stuck alone in Perth. They dutifully held her accountable by asking, "How's the book writing?" and patiently listened as Mindy tried to articulate weather learning to Doreen and Louie; Robyn and Millie; Terri, Vicky, Lola and Tess; Faye and Robbie; Helen and Bowie; and many others who sit, talk, listen and walk dogs. Mindy would also like to thank her faraway family and friends that are always patient as she works to deadlines. Thank you, Sharon Lane for your quiet and unfailing support that makes this thinking, writing and doing possible; for the epic camping trips across Western Australia; and for moving to Perth and learning how to live life together and apart in a pandemic.

Thank you to the book series editors Liselott Mariett Olsson and Michel Vandenbroeck for welcoming this contribution and to Diem Hoang for her editorial assistance.

PART I
A weather learning project

1

INTRODUCTION

Young children are growing up in a world where climate change requires us to rethink how humans should live and learn with the environment. The escalating damage to land, forests, waterways and the lives and habitats of other species across the planet requires us, as humans, to acknowledge and respond to our own part in this tragedy. For those involved in environmental education, this modern climate crisis is both a challenge and an opportunity to think more deeply about human relations with the world and the entanglement of human and nonhuman lives.

Despite a long, rich history of environmental education in early childhood education, there is still much that remains unexplored in children's relationship with climate change. As Julie Davis (2015) points out, Anthropogenic climate change is often seen as too complex, remote and difficult to include in the day-to-day education of young children; so much so, that it is often ignored rather than acknowledged as something that is already part of children's lives. In this book, we take up the challenge of bridging the divide between global climate concerns and environmental education as practiced in early years classrooms. We do this through an exploration of children's relations with weather. This is because weather is a familiar, sensory and embodied experience that is part of the everyday lives of young children. At the same time, thinking and learning with weather opens-up potential for understanding our everyday human connections to wider climatic patterns and concerns. We challenge the common assumption that positions weather as a backdrop to all human activity; and instead, bring weather to the fore (Rooney, 2019). We ask what new understandings might emerge when we see young children as learning with weather, or indeed, as also bodies of weather (Pollitt et al., 2021).

We avoid positioning climate change as a scenario that brings with it dramatic impacts that, from a somewhat remote positioning, humans must confront or

DOI: 10.4324/9781003150411-2

4 A weather learning project

bear. Rather, we focus on how our everyday human lives are entangled with weather worlds and times in ways that are inseparable from a continually changing climate. When rain washes over our skin, or dust blows in our eyes, or even when we close the doors and turn up the air conditioning, our proximity to everyday weather and wider climatic change becomes palpable. In this book, we attend to the complexities of human-weather relations and consider how this might help us to position climate change in environmental education in ways that invite connection rather than disconnection. We avoid positioning children as either the ultimate source of hope or as subject to despair in light of possible climate futures. As Donna Haraway (2016) reminds us, neither of these extremes is helpful in shaping the thinking that is needed to address the challenges of our time. The climate changes we face are happening now, not in some distant future, and so we focus on the ways children find themselves living with the uncertainties of weather in a changing climate (Haraway, 2016). It is from within the complexities of ongoing relations between humans, weather and worlds that we seek out practices and imagine alternatives for environmental learning in early childhood.

Imagining alternatives

There is little doubt that education needs to change if it is to meet the environmental challenges of our times. As a recent paper commissioned by UNESCO notes:

> In the face of the multiple existential threats, we have brought upon ourselves, business as usual is no longer an option. It is time to step up to the challenge and fundamentally reconfigure the role of education and schooling in order to radically reimagine and relearn our place and agency in the world.
>
> *(Common Worlds Research Collective, 2020, p. 2)*

The authors go on to argue that, in the context of climate change, education is suffering from a "failure to imagine alternatives" (Common Worlds Research Collective, 2020, p. 2). And further, that what is required is "a complete paradigm shift, from learning about the world in order to act upon it, to *learning to become with the world* around us. Our future survival depends on our capacity to make this shift" (Common Worlds Research Collective, 2020, p. 3) [italics in original]. It is from this starting point that we (re)imagine an approach to environmental education where children learn with weather; sensing, seeking out and forging connections with wider climate worlds, and where we notice how weather also invites children into the (re)making of new weather worlds.

We use the term *with* to emphasise interconnection and to attend to the mutual exchanges in a particular activity. To learn or think *with* weather is to adopt a positioning that is different to thinking or learning *about* weather. It is instead one where the emphasis is on relationality and mutual vulnerability, and that suggests there is something generative in the exchange between humans and weather that is worth exploring more deeply.

This book draws on findings from two ethnographic studies carried out from 2016 to 2019. The research was conducted on Ngunnawal and Ngambri Country, which has never been ceded, and we pay our respects to the First Nation custodians of this Country and its land, air and waterways. Our presence as non-Indigenous researchers is implicated in the complex colonial histories of this land which is now known as Canberra; histories that include the erasure of Indigenous weather cultures when Canberra was established and that continue to this day (Wright et al., 2021). We learn and reflect on the histories, cultures and weathers that lie deep in land and time, and acknowledge that our efforts to seek out new possibilities for shared climate worlds will inevitably be partial, imperfect, and an ongoing practice of listening and learning.

We have been fortunate to work with a wider cross-disciplinary international collective of educators and researchers through the Common Worlds Research Collective (https://commonworlds.net/) and the Climate Action Childhood Network (https://climateactionchildhood.net/). Our research was conducted with a community partner, the University Preschool Child Care Centre in Canberra, Australia. The research involved going on regular walks with educators and children in the few acres surrounding the preschool; a lightly treed, grassy, urban lakeside setting. Prior to this research, the preschool already had a strong commitment to environmental education, including an established practice of taking the children on walks outside the centre. We are indebted to the openness and trust that children, staff and families at the preschool placed in us as we experimented with new (and often uncertain) ways of engaging children with weather and outdoor worlds. We also acknowledge that our research collaborators Affrica Taylor, Felicity Royds and Jo Pollitt contributed much of the empirical and conceptual material drawn on through this book, and this book is therefore attributable to a much wider collective enterprise.

Throughout the book, we draw attention to the significance of our approach to going on walks with children, and our attempts to rethink and reposition our human relations with weather. We share findings from our field work via photos and stories, as told by adults and children. These practices act as examples for both research and pedagogy in thinking about the ways children live and learn with weather worlds. While our research is focused on children in an early years educational setting, the insights have much to offer environmental education in school years and beyond.

In this chapter, we introduce the conceptual influences that shape how we approach learning with weather and explain why we see this as an opportunity to rethink human-weather relations in environmental education. We also explain why working with weather can achieve a generative shift in early childhood

6 A weather learning project

environmental education across four main areas: redirecting the focus away from an exclusive human-centric position; resisting certainty and containment to embrace what is unknown, unbounded and unruly; responding to the ethical dimensions of human entanglements in wider climate worlds; and reimagining learning in emerging weather worlds.

Challenging human-centric perspectives and human exceptionalism

This work is situated in contemporary feminist approaches to re-thinking human relations with the world because it challenges some of the most basic assumptions of knowledge, truth and power that have underpinned modern worldviews. We engage in conversation with influences from work that might be called poststructuralist, new-materialist and posthumanist. Along with others who are leading the way in reframing early childhood education through a more-than-human lens (including Abi Hackett, Hillevi Lenz Taguchi, Fikile Nxumalo, Veronica Pacini-Ketchabaw, Pauliina Rautio, Margaret Somerville, Affrica Taylor and others), we propose that a significant shift is required if teachers are to develop pedagogies that move beyond the artificial binaries of nature-culture, and (in our work) human-weather, that cannot be sustained.

In the face of climate change, it has become increasingly evident that the tradition of humanism, and its reliance on human-centric positioning in relation to how we come to know, think of and act on the world, is now well and truly not working. The disasters and tragedies of human-induced climate change show that if we live with a worldview where humans are at the centre, then (whether inadvertently or not) this can perpetuate a positioning of human exceptionalism, where dominance, neglect, exploitation or disregard for nonhuman worlds comes with far-reaching impacts. This clearly does not make sense when humans rely on the environment for food, shelter and clothing; yet, to only focus on the implications for humans is once again to bring humans and their future fortunes to the centre. Here we do not ignore the significant impact on human lives, and the fact that some human lives are more considerably and unevenly impacted than others by the unfolding disasters of a changing climate. We do however extend our concern and interest to all lives, ecologies, matters and times to consider how young children's learning in a climate change era might promote recognition, responsiveness and transformation within these wider more-than-human worlds.[1]

In reflecting on the scholarly tradition of Western philosophical thought, Val Plumwood (2002) draws attention to the cultural pattern of *hyperseparation* that is embedded in binary dualisms such as culture/nature, subject/object and mind/body, noting that these artificial power structures work to posit humans as superior. According to Plumwood, it is precisely these structures that have led to denial of the ecological crisis that we face; one that is "not just or even primarily a crisis of technology, but is rather a crisis of rationality, morality and imagination" (2002, pp. 97–98). Deborah Bird Rose (2018) also challenges the

Introduction **7**

constructed myth of hyperseparation, drawing attention to connectivity and interactivity within ecology:

> The most profound insight from ecology is that humans are not hyperseparated. We are part of the biosphere. The illusion of mastery and control is exactly that: an illusion … We are inside the biosphere, and we are participants, for better and (increasingly) for worse.
>
> *(p. 495)*

The project of destabilising and questioning culture/nature and other binaries, and the power differences inherent in these structures, is among other things a feminist project; a point we return to in more detail in the next chapter. It is also a project of recognising that dualisms are constructs that, although they attempt to be universal, belong only to a particular time and school of thought. In contrast, notions of connectivity and interdependence are, as Rose (2018) reminds us, "domains in which many Indigenous people have been living for millennia" (p. 495), and thus there is much to learn by looking beyond both rigid boundaries and positions that privilege humans as central to world-making.

Learning that resists certainty and containment

The practice of education often involves packaging up knowledge as certain and contained. Working with concepts that are uncertain or only partially formed, or that remain open and unanswered, is not generally encouraged. Throughout this book, we return to themes that challenge notions of certainty and containment, arguing that environmental education can only get so far with this type of framing that – while often used for convenience in planning lessons – will not serve the more open learning that children need in the face of a changing climate. In our work with young children, we notice that much early childhood teaching about weather tends to focus on elements such as sunshine, rain, clouds, wind and snow. And while these are not always comfortable weathers, they are often presented as discrete phenomena that are in themselves somehow singular and at times romanticised. For example, typical examples of weather-related activities for young children might include the following: (1) viewing the elements of the weather while outside and then sketching what is seen; (2) using a digital camera to take photographs of the elements of weather; (3) comparing these photographs of weather with those found on the internet; (4) constructing weather cards from the digital photographs and internet research; (5) using these weather cards during their outdoor play to keep an eye on the weather to see if they can match any of the components to their weather cards (adapted from Campbell et al., 2018, pp. 276–277). There is little mention of more discomforting or less visible connections such as the idea that wind might be mingled with pollution, bushfire smoke or airborne viruses, or that rain run-off might carry waste as far as the ocean, even though it is increasingly clear that these are everyday environmental

8 A weather learning project

phenomena. When weather is discussed in early childhood education settings, it is usually in terms of whether it might be good or bad for outdoor play, or discussing what the weather is outside during the morning weather wheel routine (Rooney et al., 2021). Sometimes teachers do use these moments to reflect on the mutual vulnerabilities that humans and other species might face in increasingly hotter, drier or wetter seasons. Such conversations can help to show how there is rarely anything innocent about a gentle breeze or a shower of rain, even though these can be nurturing and life-giving. It is these types of less easily contained and more open conversations and conceptualisations of weather that are of interest to us because they offer opportunities to grapple with our relations with these weather worlds and how we can respond.

Although education frameworks tend to present and promote ideas about knowledge in certain and contained ways, young children seem to have a strong willingness to work with uncertainty and the uncontainable. For example, some children love to play in mud for hours, or to invent games that are free and evolving. Many teachers who work with young children understand that this kind of open-ended, inventive, sensory and messy play, that is not directed towards any predetermined or even knowable outcome, is significant across many areas of child development (Fleer, 2021). On our walks, we have noticed that young children are often more interested in questions rather than answers and tend to invoke imaginative speculation in wondering about the world, rather than having a need for neatly framed or bounded solutions. We have also noticed that children tend to linger at various spots. They are curious and slow down to investigate odd things, rather than simply rushing on to a destination. We share lots of evidence of these ways of learning and suggest that working with young children is thus the ideal setting from which to rethink environmental education more broadly. Drawing attention to the curiosity of young children also acts as a reminder to challenge approaches to early childhood education that tend to resist the learning potential of working with what is unknown, unbounded and unruly.

By focusing on learning that attends to all manner of both anticipated and erratic weather, and by being curious about weather affects as it mingles with bodies, lives and matter, we hope to show that there are ways of knowing and imagining with weather that do not necessarily fit within contained and structured lesson planning, and yet which foster connection and responsiveness to changing climate patterns and worlds.

Ethical entanglements

Approaching environmental education through the lens of child-weather relations also provides an opportunity to focus on the ethical demands that come from living in complex, changing and challenging climate worlds. We live in a world shared with more-than-human others, and yet so much human activity continues to be destructive rather than restorative, defensive rather than responsive, and is also largely focused on human-centred needs and concerns. This raises several questions that we continue to pursue through this book:

- How can we live well together with more-than-human others in the climate worlds we inhabit together, and what responsibilities does this entail?
- How might we envisage learning that is ethically responsive and open to ways of living with others, including multi-species ecologies and ecosystems?
- How might learning with weather help to foster learning that is deeply connected and responsive to the climate challenges of our time?
- How might strategies such as listening to weather offer ways of thinking differently about human–weather relations?

In this book, we look at how ethical engagement involves more than learning *about* things, and rather requires a willingness to (un)think and (un)learn, to challenge the framings we (adults) have grown up with and take for granted, and to shift our orientation to learning *with* worlds. To do this, we need a different way of thinking about human/environment relations – to imagine education anew in ways that respond to climate change challenges. We show how the things we do not know can still be generative when taken up in speculative thinking and doing (Haraway, 2013). Within early childhood education settings, there are choices to be made about what matters in the approach to learning practices and pedagogies; choices that inevitably have political and ethical dimensions. As education practice continues to evolve and foster children's connections with what is happening in wider weather worlds, it must also attend to possibilities for responsiveness and care in the context of climate change and consider what this means for pedagogy and practice.

Imagining weather worlds together

This book is not just about finding different ways of thinking, it is a project of doing, walking, writing, making and becoming with weather as an example of environmental learning. We acknowledge the catastrophic reality that climate change is bringing to Earth, and in response, focus on what we can do in our work with children in the here-ish and the now-ish (Povinelli, 2016). We also situate this work as one small part of collective world making that continues with children, weather and more-than-human lives and places. In terms of environmental education, we are not striving to create a neat toolkit or weather curriculum to share how we might teach children *about* weather. Rather we consider how weather learning (as learning with weather) can help us in our work with children to imagine and speculate in ways that are generative of responsiveness and responsibility in a climate change context. When we talk of responsiveness in this book, we often refer to human responsiveness in relation to more-than-human worlds. However, this is not to suggest that responsiveness only comes from humans. As Anna Tsing reminds us, it is perfectly reasonable

10 A weather learning project

to consider the ways nonhumans respond to each other, such as in worlds where nonhumans might thrive without us, or to otherwise seek out ways we might think about the "responses of the many, each to each other, rather than just to response-seeking humans" (Tsing, 2019, p. 225). While we attempt this, for example, through imagining the vitality and world making between weather and multi-species others, we agree this is not easy work. As Tsing says, "the challenge is to appreciate the dynamism of the other-than-human world without imagining facts that speak for themselves" (p. 230). Shifts such as these can act as an attempt to resist the many ways we tend to privilege human action as central to addressing climate change challenges. Imagining weather worlds together can therefore be a human and more-than-human collective happening. To imagine – and to speculate – is not just to think about the future, but is about the actions and happenings in our ordinary lives that are always open, always in-progress, and thus generative of multiple possible weather worlds. The challenge is to imagine worlds that are better for all lives and ecologies in going-on together. This involves becoming-with others and turning to what is still possible in recuperation (Haraway, 2016).

Rethinking environmental education through learning with weather

To rethink environmental education through the four shifts described above – moving beyond human-centrism, learning with what is uncertain, uncontained and unruly, responding to our ethical entanglements with climate worlds, and reimagining weather worlds together – we adopt an approach that is centred on an exploration of children's relations with weather as a way of understanding how children learn, live and become with wider weather worlds. By foregrounding weather in children's experiences, we draw attention to weather as material, embodied, affective and generative of and with children's worldly encounters. Thus, we explicitly theorise *weather* in our conceptualisation of both worlds and materiality. We attend to the threads of connection that extend between children and weather to better understand wider climate relations.

Several scholars have inspired our thinking on the connections between climate and weather. Astrida Neimanis and Rachel Walker (2014) invited us to think differently about bodies and weather, Tim Ingold (2015) talks of the inseparability of humans from weather and introduced us to the notion of *weather worlds* and Phillip Vannini and others (2012) drew our attention to the sensory connections between bodies, place and weather. This body of scholarship influenced earlier foundational work undertaken by Rooney (2018; 2019) on how we might start to rethink the relations between young children and weather in environmental education, and the collaborative work we have carried out since towards developing new weather pedagogies (Blaise & Rooney, 2019; Pollitt et al., 2021; Rooney et al., 2021). More recently, we have engaged with the writing of the Bawaka collective (Burarrwanga et al., 2019; Bawaka Collective,

Introduction **11**

2021), which has further challenged us to think differently about the relationship between land, time, colonisation and weather.

Weather is everything. Understanding how we came to this idea – and the unexpected and life-giving collaborations that we found along the way – provides unique insight into human relations with worlds of climate and weather. As we argue in this book, a focus on children's weather relations brings with it the potential to frame an approach to environmental education that will hopefully support ways of living and learning better with weather and climate as a way of weathering together with human and more-than-human companions in a challenging climate change era.

There are possibilities, challenges and tensions in the work we do. One of the tensions we tackle includes attuning to the specific ways in which children experience and respond to weather worlds while at the same time trying to avoid positioning the child as a central point of focus, as is often the tendency in education practice. This is because we want to challenge the dominance of human-centric positioning in a climate change context; though as is inevitable in this work, we still recognise our own perspective as a human one. In reflecting on the work of Pauliina Rautio (2021), we think of this as one of many *balancing acts* that we juggle in this book. Another is the tension between a desire for clarity in our thinking while leaving room for uncertainty. This a balancing act Rautio (2021) explains as one:

> between being able to say something, or speak for something, and highlighting the complexity and entanglement of everything and being in the world. The more stubborn the focus on representation as something, the less space there is for the not-yet-known, the emerging, the wild, the uncategorizable.
>
> *(p. 229)*

We want to make space here for what emerges, no matter how ordinary or wild it seems.

In Part I, we situate the significance of this project theoretically, empirically and most importantly in the context of the climate change era in which young children are learning. This chapter provides an introduction and in Chapter 2 we briefly survey contemporary research in environmental education and related fields. This situates the book within wider discussions on climate change and young children. From there, the book is structured around three practices: methods, relations and responses.

In Part II, we discuss our research methods and the potential these have for a different approach to pedagogical thinking and practice. Over three chapters, we consider the actions of thinking with weather, walking with weather and writing with weather. We discuss the significance of these as feminist methods and practices, and demonstrate both the research and pedagogical potential of these for environmental education. In Chapter 3, we think with weather, expanding

12 A weather learning project

on four concepts that have helped us to think differently about weather: weather worlds, weather bodies, weather place-making and weathering together. Our thinking traverses time, space and culture, adding new insights that take us beyond everyday thinking about weather. In Chapter 4, we move with weather. Specifically, we describe our research methods and practices with children as a form of walking with weather and draw attention to the pedagogical potential of walking as a form of learning. In Chapter 5, we turn to our practice of writing and explain how we have nurtured our writing craft to navigate between thinking and doing which we see as much entwined. We show how and why we tell small weather stories that both challenge and cultivate ways that we might rethink human-weather relations and responsibilities.

In Part III, we turn to the multitude of weather relations that we have noticed in our research and how children might learn with and through these. In Chapter 6, we explore children's relations both with and as weather bodies and consider the affective experience of children's encounters with other types of weather bodies. In Chapter 7, we then turn to children's weather relations via multi-species encounters with plants, animals and complex ecological systems, including what these bring to children's ideas of life, death, extinction and mutual vulnerability. In Chapter 8, we consider human weather relations through deeper concepts of space and time that extend beyond the here and now of our time and place on Earth.

Finally, in Part IV, we consider why weather learning is important in environmental education if we are to develop and put into practice responsive and generative pedagogies in a climate change era. In Chapter 9, we draw together various threads of our discussion on teaching and learning to highlight key practices and strategies for implementing an approach to learning with weather in early childhood and environmental education. Finally, in Chapter 10, we open an invitation to continue the practice of weather learning. We consider the potential of speculation in making weather worlds together and reflect on the possibilities for care in shaping better and more liveable worlds.

There are many spaces that we cannot fill or reach in this book. Working and thinking with weather has helped us to understand that the extent of what is not-yet-known, and what is increasingly wild or unprecedented, is significant and not to be ignored if we are to grapple with climate change in contemporary education. It is with this in mind that we embark on a discussion that moves between scholarly debate, stories from our fieldwork with children and speculation as to the shape of environmental learning that might be best placed to tackle the climate challenges of our times.

Note

1 We follow human geographers and environmental humanities scholars who use the term more-than-human to indicate plant and animal species, elements, forces, ancestral knowledges and more. For us, "more-than-human" does not mean better than or "above" the human, but rather "more-than-human" is expansive and makes room for difference and the presence of multispecies.

References

Bawaka Collective. (2021). *Bawaka Collective: Both ways learning.* Bawaka Collective. https://bawakacollective.com/

Blaise, M., & Rooney, T. (2019). Listening to and telling a rush of unruly natureculture gender stories. In F. Nxumalo & C. P. Brown (Eds.), *Disrupting and countering deficits in early childhood education* (pp. 151–163). Routledge. http://doi.org/10.4324/9781315102696-10

Burarrwanga, L., Ganambarr, R., Ganambarr-Stubbs, M., Ganambarr, B., Maymuru, D., Wright, S. L., Suchet-Pearson, S., & Lloyd, K. (2019). *Songspirals: Sharing women's wisdom of Country through songlines.* Allen & Unwin.

Campbell, C., Jobling, W., & Howitt, C. (Eds.). (2018). *Science in early childhood.* Cambridge University Press.

Common Worlds Research Collective. (2020). *Learning to become with the world: Education for future survival.* UNESCO. https://unesdoc.unesco.org/ark:/48223/pf0000374923

Davis, J. (Ed.). (2015). *Young children and the environment: Early education for sustainability* (2nd ed.). Cambridge University Press.

Fleer, M. (2021). *Play in the early years* (3rd ed.). Cambridge University Press. https://doi.org/10.1017/9781108908153

Haraway, D. (2013). SF: Science fiction, speculative fabulation, string figures, so far. *Ada: A Journal of Gender, New Media, and Technology, 11*(3), 1–18. http://doi.org/10.7264/N3KH0K81

Haraway, D. (2016). *Staying with the trouble: Making kin in the Chthulucene.* Duke University Press.

Ingold, T. (2015). *The life of lines.* Routledge.

Neimanis, A., & Walker, R. L. (2014). Weathering: Climate change and the 'thick time' of transcorporeality. *Hypatia, 29*(3), 558–575. https://doi.org/10.1111/hypa.12064

Plumwood, V. (2002). *Environmental culture: The ecological crisis of reason.* Routledge.

Pollitt, J., Blaise, M., & Rooney, T. (2021). Weather bodies: Experimenting with dance improvisation in environmental education in the early years. *Environmental Education Research, 27*(8), 1141–1151. https://doi.org/10.1080/13504622.2021.1926434

Povinelli, E. (2016). *Geontologies: A Requiem to late liberalism.* Duke University Press.

Rautio, P. (2021). Post-qualitative inquiry: Four balancing acts in crafting alternative stories to live by. *Qualitative Inquiry, 27*(2), 228–230. https://doi.org/10.1177/1077800420933297

Rooney, T. (2018). Weather worlding: Learning with the elements in early childhood. *Environmental Education Research, 24*(1), 1–12. https://doi.org/10.1080/13504622.2016.1217398

Rooney, T. (2019). Weathering time: Walking with young children in a changing climate. *Children's Geographies, 17*(2), 177–189. https://doi.org/10.1080/14733285.2018.1474172

Rooney, T., Blaise, M., & Royds, F. (2021). With shadows, dust and mud: Activating weathering-with pedagogies in early childhood education. *Contemporary Issues in Early Childhood, 22*(2), 109–123. https://doi.org/10.1177%2F1463949120939202

Rose, D. B. (2018). Connectivity thinking, animism, and the pursuit of liveliness. *Educational Theory, 67*(4), 491–508. https://doi.org/10.1111/edth.12260

Tsing, A. L. (2019). When the things we study respond to each other: Tools for unpacking "the material". In P. Harvey, C. Krohn-Hansen, & K. G. Nustad (Eds.), *Anthropos and the material* (pp. 221–243). Duke University Press. https://www.dukeupress.edu/anthropos-and-the-material

14 A weather learning project

Vannini, P., Waskul, D., Gottschalk, S., & Ellis-Newstead, T. (2012). Making sense of the weather: Dwelling and weathering on Canada's rain coast. *Space and Culture, 15*(4), 361–380. https://doi.org/10.1177%2F1206331211412269

Wright, S., Daley, L., & Curtis, F. (2021). Weathering colonisation: Aboriginal resistance and survivance in the siting of the capital. In K. Barry, M. Borovnik & T. Edensor (Eds.), *Weather: Spaces, mobilities and affects* (pp. 207–221). Routledge.

2
YOUNG CHILDREN AND ENVIRONMENTAL EDUCATION

This first half of this chapter charts some of the rich history of environmental education in early childhood and related disciplines of childhood studies and children's geographies. These three fields are in many ways inseparable. Together, they get to the heart of how we think about children, both within education systems and in the wider worlds they inhabit. Childhood studies, for example, focuses on children and society and related concepts such as agency, while the field of children's geographies investigates children's relationship with space, time and place. Children live with a multitude of other beings (human and nonhuman) with whom they share spaces, histories, cultures and politics that shape their relations and futures. The practice of education is grounded in a philosophy of thinking about the relationship between children, learning and the learning environment. More traditional theories tend to posit learning and the environment as separate and discrete entities, while recent approaches seek out ways in which these might be mutually co-constitutive, such as the Reggio Emilia approach to recognising learning spaces or environments as the "third teacher" (Rinaldi, 2006, p. 77). Bringing together insights from these cross-disciplinary perspectives can help to inform different ways we might think about children's learning within and with learning environments.

The second half of this chapter explains the significance of the shift towards postdevelopmental approaches to learning, which act as a starting point for the directions in environmental education set out in this book. Finally, we introduce our approach to rethinking human relations with more-than-human worlds through conceptual influences from feminism and environmental humanities.

DOI: 10.4324/9781003150411-3

16 A weather learning project

Cross-disciplinary influences – Childhood studies and children's geographies

In addition to the field of education, the disciplines of childhood studies and children's geographies inform the broader context for the ways children and childhood are understood and discussed in this book. Both fields represent influential bodies of work of increasing relevance for environmental education. Over the past few decades, these areas of research have contributed to reconceptualising notions of agency, innocence and becoming (childhood studies) as well as children's relationship with space, movement, time and place (children's geographies).

While the notion of childhood might seem straightforward, it has remained highly contentious (James et al., 1998), with ongoing debate as to how to conceptualise children in relation to society (Jenks, 2005), agency and adulthood (James et al., 1998), nature (Taylor, 2013), technology (Yelland, 2007) and the future (Prout, 2005). Children have at times been viewed as passive and at the whim of being shaped by adults and the environment. One of the significant shifts that childhood studies scholars have brought to the fore is the idea that children are active in the construction and determination of their own lives (Jenks, 2005). As part of this, scholars such as Nick Lee (2001) and Alan Prout (2005) have questioned the binary distinction between adult/child and public/private spheres. For example, they and others call into question the idea that child development is linear with clearly defined stages and challenge the deficit model that is often applied to children in relation to adults, highlighting instead the contextual and diverse factors that are entwined with children's becoming with the world. The idea that children should only be understood in relation to family and home life is also challenged, and in response children's lives are positioned as well and truly both social and political (Prout, 2005). If we consider children in relation to nature, at various times in history children have alternately been portrayed as wild, untamed and therefore congruent with nature, or pure and innocent and yet puzzlingly also congruent with nature (Jenks, 2005). Affrica Taylor's work on refiguring the relationship between nature and childhood makes a shift beyond these tensions, to reposition children as neither aligned with or in nature by highlighting how such a positioning relies on a binary that separates nature from culture (Taylor, 2013, 2017); concepts we return to later in this chapter.

In children's geographies, there is considerable research on the importance of children being understood as active social participants and having the opportunity to explore the outdoors and move freely through their local environment. One well-established field of research is on children's independent mobility which draws attention to how the capacity of children is often underestimated, and as a result, also overly controlled (Bourke, 2017; Freeman & Tranter, 2011; Hickey & Phillips, 2013; Malone & Rudner, 2011; Valentine & McKendrick, 1997). A brief overview of these ideas is provided by John Horton et al. (2014), who expand on how these ideas have shaped the contemporary field of children's

Young children and environmental education **17**

geographies. Some researchers in this field draw attention to the political and power structures that are imbued in public spaces (Katz, 2001; Valentine, 2004) often in ways that are designed to control or limit children's movement and participation in society, and the subsequent forms of resistance that both children and adults might raise to counter such structures. This body of research highlights how space is not simply an objective or passive structure, nor a container for social relations and events. Instead, space is active and plays a role constituting identities and vice versa. The relationship between children and environments, and the co-constitution of spaces, is pursued further throughout this book.

The cross-disciplinary influences described above help to shift our thinking beyond questions of children's place in society, to examine the relationship between children and environment, and the interactions, power relations and connections that shape this experience.

Environmental education – Origins in outdoor play and learning

Environmental education in early childhood education has a long history. In many respects, educators working with young children have been at the forefront of practices that recognise the significance of outdoor learning and children's relationship with the natural world (Cutter-Mackenzie et al., 2014), and this field of research continues to be influential in environmental education more broadly.

First, a note on terminology. Throughout the book, we use the term *environmental education* in preference to other terms such as education for sustainability or climate change education. We recognise the overlap between these endeavours. In brief, we avoid the term sustainability where it might be conflated with sustainable development because of the emphasis in this field on the sustainability of human futures; not that this is unimportant, but our interest in children's relations with more-than-human worlds tends to get lost in this discourse. We also feel sustainability is not strong enough as the Earth is now so damaged that more is needed than to simply sustain what we have. We need to recuperate, restore, reimagine and rethink what flourishing lives for *all* creatures might look like. The field of education for sustainability has however played a significant role in drawing attention to issues of social justice, inequity and power; all of which are critical in shaping new and fairer climate worlds (Davis, 2015), and is thus a vital body of work that we engage with in this book. The term climate change education (Rousell & Cutter-Mackenzie-Knowles, 2020) is also closely related to the work we do; however, it focuses more on school-based pedagogies and does not capture the full range of interconnected environmental issues and phenomena that we wish to discuss. The term environmental education, even though one of the earlier terms in the field, thus keeps us grounded – historically and literally – and seems to most broadly encompass what has been a long and evolving discourse on the relationship between children, learning

18 A weather learning project

and environments (Gough, 2016). Critically, for us, there is no human versus environment. Humans are always and already part of environments that include ecologies, places, times, species, processes, atmospheres and geologies. Similarly, the education practice we discuss is not education *about* the world, but rather a variety of practices of doing, thinking, responding, imagining and learning *with* worlds. These are themes we expand on throughout this book.

In both historical and contemporary research, educators from a range of philosophical positions have recognised that providing children with access to outdoor environments brings benefits for learning and development, as well as social, physical and emotional wellbeing. For example, outdoor spaces promote children's health through increased physical activity (Sharma-Brymer & Bland, 2016), provide affordances for risky play (Gill, 2007; Sandseter, 2009) and offer open-ended spaces and materials that encourage free play driven by children's curiosity and imagination (Flannigan & Dietze, 2018). An increase in the opportunities for outdoor and risky play has emerged as a response to children spending longer hours indoors, drawing attention to the benefits for children's health, wellbeing, connection to nature and sensory learning (Beery & Jørgensen, 2018). Outdoor learning is significant for environmental education. Some suggest that access to the outdoors helps to foster appreciation and respect for the natural world, and that without this, children can experience disconnection with negative impacts on wellbeing (Louv, 2005). Opportunities for outdoor learning can be enacted specifically through curriculum, or more informally through other forms of play and learning. Outdoor activities might be part of a daily routine, or more fully embedded in the overarching philosophy or physical design of a preschool or early learning centre; for example, through outdoor environments designed to promote movement (Merewether, 2015), connection to place and community (Rooney, 2015) or exploration and risk taking (Little et al., 2017).

Recent decades have seen a rise in the numbers of forest schools, bush kinders and other forms of nature education in early childhood learning centres, including across the United Kingdom, Scandinavia and Australia (Elliott & Chancellor, 2014; Mycock, 2020; Sandseter, 2014). In the United Kingdom, Katherine Mycock (2020) reports how forest schools emerged in the 1990s, with numbers continuing to expand to this day. The children in these schools visit the same outdoor nature place over time, usually accompanied by a qualified forest school-teacher (Mycock, 2020). Given the decades over which these schools have been running, it is not surprising that we might witness a range of pedagogical approaches and shifts in environmental learning across this period. However, as Mycock (2020) observes, there is still a tendency to maintain child-centred or anthropocentric approaches to learning. Building on the UK forest school model, bush and beach kinder programs in Australia have also grown in popularity, with hundreds now running across the country. A similar feature of these programs is that the children and educators regularly spend time each day or week in a bush setting near the preschool or early learning centre engaging in long periods of unstructured and child-directed play (Elliott & Chancellor, 2014). The learning potential of these spaces has been recognised as significant for opening up new possibilities for sustainability and science education (Campbell & Speldewinde, 2020), with more recent studies pointing to the opportunities that bush kinders provide to rethink the ways that children learn with nature and to experience weather and seasonal changes (Grogan & Hughes, 2020). In Scandinavia, the early childhood education curriculum encourages outdoor and nature play as vital for children's wellbeing, development and learning across all early childhood learning; and there is also a shift to establish specific outdoor preschools that use natural environments as the primary learning space (Sandseter & Hagen, 2016). Finally, we note the influence of the Reggio Emilia approach to learning in early childhood, which from its Italian origins has been adopted world-wide. This approach elevates the significance of the environment as a key partner in children's learning, prompting the teacher to create flexible environments that promote curiosity and learning (Rinaldi, 2006).

Programs, such as those described above, continue to evolve and highlight the significance of outdoor learning for environmental education. Add to this the range of school and community garden programs that engage children in growing food and thinking about food sources, seasonality and soil systems, and we get a sense of the breadth and depth of environmental learning opportunities in early childhood education (Davis, 2015; Edwards & Cutter-Mackenzie, 2011; Elliott et al., 2020). While not all environmental learning takes place outdoors, and there is not always a clear indoor/outdoor divide associated with particular pedagogies, there is no doubt that outdoor learning continues to have a central role.

Environmental education and child development

We do not wish to duplicate here the already expansive breadth of research on early childhood environmental education, and instead highlight some of the comprehensive literature reviews that have been undertaken in recent years. Taken together, these reviews go a long way to providing an overview of the work undertaken in this field. For example, the literature reviews on education for sustainability by Tülin Güler Yıldız et al. (2021) and education for sustainable development by Maria Hedefalk et al. (2015) chart the use of these approaches in early childhood education contexts over the past couple of decades and highlight the transformative potential of action-based approaches to teaching for environmental change. Margaret Somerville and Carolyn Williams (2015), building on an earlier review by Julie Davis (2009), also survey the research on sustainability education, though with more emphasis on the range of methodological and theoretical orientations that emerged across this body of work. This review is particularly helpful in identifying the significance of the relationship between children and the environment while also highlighting the ways this is often considered out of scope in reviews on environmental education. In this book, we too draw on material on child/environment relations that may have been missed in more structured literature reviews on environmental education. In a report for the NSW Environmental Trust, Sue Elliott et al. (2016) give a comprehensive overview of literature on environmental education that also encompasses sustainability education. For research with a specific emphasis on climate change education, both Martha C. Monroe et al. (2019) and David Rousell and Amy Cutter-Mackenzie-Knowles (2020) provide insightful reviews of literature in the context of anthropogenic climate change.

Thus, for readers interested in getting a sense of the depth and breadth of literature in this field, there is no shortage of material. In our own reading, we have noticed that broadening our literature searches to include *early childhood education* together with terms such as *anthropocene* or *nature-culture divide* surfaces a whole additional body of work (such as, for example, Duhn et al., 2017; Somerville, 2017) that is not captured in many of the reviews mentioned above. In general, much of this additional work extends the theoretical paradigm from a child *development* perspective to a *postdevelopmental* paradigm. In this book, we adopt a postdevelopmental approach, which is not to suggest that this should replace child development approaches to learning, as these remains foundational to early childhood education practice today. Rather, we focus on postdevelopmental perspectives because they allow us to turn our gaze differently to particular matters or concerns using concepts and methods that are not possible within a traditional child development framework.

As an example of the shift we adopt, consider the systematic literature review by Nicole Ardoin and Alison Bowers (2020) that provides a review of 66 early childhood environmental education programs. In assessing the programs, the outcomes are framed by domains of children's development, including environmental literacy development, cognitive development, social and emotional development, physical development and language and literacy development. The study finds that 76% of the programs reviewed showed evidence of improvement in children's environmental literacy development (these indicators were related to environmental knowledge, understandings, attitude and skills and behaviours that would inform decision making related to taking care of the environment). This study demonstrates the benefits of environmental education programs across all areas of children's learning and development. In contrast, the goal of our ethnographic research on child–weather relations is not related to improving or better understanding the development or growth of individual children. Rather our interest is in children's encounters and relations with place, and other species and phenomena, specifically weather, and the affective, bodily and situated dimensions of children's learning that happens in these encounters. Researchers using a child development paradigm would certainly arrive at findings of interest via the walking methods we use. For example, our methods could be adapted to assess the impact on children's science literacy in how children come to understand species life–cycles, or children's physical agility as they scramble over rocks and climb in the low branches of trees. The change in children's confidence in navigating the outdoors may also be of interest. In anecdotal terms, we have seen changes in development across these areas, and some evidence of this may be gleaned incidentally from the stories we share. However, we do not report on these aspects here as this is not the focus of the design or aims of our study.

As explained in more detail below, we position our gaze through a postdevelopmental lens so that we can look beyond the framings that often separate learning and development into distinct domains. This also provides a positioning from which to imagine, speculate and generate other possible weather knowledges and worlds; an approach that we argue is vital in the context of climate change, which (as noted earlier) requires a radical rethink of human relations with the environment if we are to respond in ways that will make a difference.

Early childhood education and postdevelopmentalism

Postdevelopmentalism in early childhood education provides conceptual, methodological and pedagogical opportunities for rethinking environmental education in the context of a changing climate. In this section, we briefly outline the elements in the shift to postdevelopmentalism that are of most relevance to our research. Postdevelopmentalism has made its presence felt in education studies through the convergence of several wider debates. We outline three of these briefly here.

Firstly, there is a shift in conceptualisations of children and childhood mentioned earlier from passive to active in shaping their own agency. While traditional child development theorists articulate childhood as a state of *becoming* that moves along an expected trajectory of development or growth, usually towards a state that is more complete or advanced, these are notions that have been challenged by scholars who see the child as socially constituted by culture, and as having agency in their own right (that is, *being*) not just in respect of the adult they will *become*. We can see similar shifts in other aspects of child development that have traditionally centred around binary logics; for example, the division between male/female or boy/girl which for so long has created bias and limitations in the views that teachers and parents have about children's capacity and interests. Feminist and postdevelopmental thinking opened new directions that allowed for more fluid and complex ideas about gender (Blaise, 2005; Blaise, 2010; Blaise & Rooney, 2020). Education theorists working with socio-cultural theory also acknowledge the significance of context and experience, though with variation in views as to what this means for child development (e.g. Lee, 2001; Prout, 2005). One common theme across these works is a shift to seeing children and young people as agents of change. This trajectory can be seen in relation to recent climate change activism where young people, such as Swedish climate activist Greta Thunberg, are increasingly taking the lead and no longer excusing adult inaction (Verlie & Flynn, 2022).

Secondly, we also notice changes in the conceptualisation of the child in relation to other beings and matters. For example, Taylor (2013) challenges the

22 A weather learning project

ways we think about the relationship between children and nature, refiguring children's relations with the world as entangled naturecultures, expanding on this further in a co-authored book examining child-animal relations (Taylor & Pacini-Ketchabaw, 2015). Key to this work is an understanding that in early childhood education, it is not just children that have agency:

> As we see it, the children are not the only orchestrators or actors in these interspecies worlds and encounters. Rather, the learning emerges from the relations taking place between all the actors – human and more-than-human alike.
>
> *(Taylor & Pacini-Ketchabaw, 2015, p. 3)*

As a further example, Hillevi Lenz Taguchi's (2010) scholarship on agential realism in early childhood education offers new insights into young children's relations with everyday materials. Common to these works is a challenging of preconceived boundaries between child and nature, child and materiality and theory and practice to consider a more entangled and co-constitutive notion of being, existence and knowledge (see also Ceder, 2019; Kraftl, 2020; Pacini-Ketchabaw et al., 2016a).

Applying postdevelopmental ideas in early childhood education leads to pedagogies that emphasise method and process alongside the acquisition of content and knowledge. This gives us tools to consider how we might shift perspectives and decentre the human in educational practice (Pacini-Ketchabaw et al., 2016b). Also of significance is the collective approach to research and education that surrounds this new work. For example, the Common Worlds Research Collective (established by Veronica Pacini-Ketchabaw, Affrica Taylor and Mindy Blaise) turns to the significance of shared or common worlds as being those worlds that children inhabit with more-than-human others, and the importance of collective and generative thinking and doing in shaping these worlds (Pacini-Ketchabaw et al., 2016b).

Finally, another point of convergence between postdevelopmental approaches to early childhood education and wider issues is in coming to understand the potential in bringing anti-colonial, postcolonial and decolonising perspectives and practices to education. In Fikile Nxumalo's book *Decolonising Place in Early Childhood Education* (2019), she discusses how the dominance of Western thought in educational practice has hardened the child-nature divide, and yet this is a divide that that has been and still is – across both histories and other cultures – not at all significant in wider ways of thinking or knowing the world. Nxumalo (2019) argues therefore, that to work in ways that disrupt binaries is not a project that involves disrupting a truth that always has been – but rather, it is to work at disrupting structures that were established within the foundations of Western thought as convenient, political and power-motivated frameworks. As educators and researchers, to adopt a postdevelopmental lens to educational practice and pedagogy is also to acknowledge, question and dismantle the historical and colonial underpinnings of our practice that might continue to serve the interests of a few at the expense of silencing others. In this book, we turn to the perspectives of Indigenous scholars, such as those in the Bawaka Collective (Bawaka Country et al., 2015) who have helped to draw our attention to the colonial underpinnings that are often present in education practice, including in our own teaching and research on environment and weather.

These features described above are all themes that we expand on more fully throughout this book. We use the term postdevelopmental to indicate that we are situating this scholarship in something more than child development, developmental psychology or human capital theories. Postdevelopmentalism is part of a broad worldview that challenges the basic tenets of the regulatory forces of modernism, such as the notion of a single and stable truth; the possibility of objective and value-free knowledge; the desire for linearity; and the functionality of either/or thinking. Postdevelopmentalism values complexities, multiplicities, subjectivities, contexts, provisionalities and uncertainties (Dahlberg et al., 1999). We want to understand and produce a pedagogical project that is different from the dominant one. The tools and ideas offered by postdevelopmentalism allow us to take our thinking on early childhood environmental education beyond the constraints of modernism to consider more relational, embodied and situated notions of knowledge and practice.

Postdevelopmentalism draws from all sorts of perspectives including poststructuralism, postcolonialism, Indigenous studies, Black studies, queer theory, feminisms, new materialisms, posthumanisms and so on. We turn now to briefly explain the significance of some of these wider influences that have challenged us to think differently about child-environment relations.

Wider influences – Feminism and environmental humanities

Alongside the significant new directions in environmental education and early childhood education, we are also influenced by wider scholarship that explores human relationships with more-than-human worlds in the context of climate change. This work helps us to reconceptualise our thinking on children's relations with other species, with place and temporalities and with weathers and climate. In this section, we briefly explain how and why we have been influenced by both feminist scholarship and recent work in the environmental humanities.

This book is a feminist project. Along with the multiple and diverse concepts that have emerged in the short history of feminism since the 1900s, feminist thinking has consistently challenged traditional Western (usually male) notions of bodies, binaries, hierarchies and power. A feminist project does not only work to challenge and unravel the binary structures that for so long have reinforced unjust power imbalances (for example between mind/body, adult/child, man/woman and human/nature), it more importantly works to create and invent worlds. As Julie MacLeavy et al. discuss, feminist theory is not a static or singular movement, but one "which has the vitality to animate social change

24 A weather learning project

through open-ended invention and the desire to bring a different future into existence" (2021, p. 16).

In the context of climate change, the damage being done by a world of activity that places human progress at the centre – and that plunders resources with a certain sense of entitlement – only serves to highlight the problems inherent in a view that places humans above and separate from nature. Creating and opening spaces for thinking differently about human-world relations, and for questioning the integrity and purpose of other binary structures, is therefore one key to shifting the drivers that underpin human action in relation to others, other species, and worlds that are made together. Feminist thinking also highlights the dangers of ideologies grounded in certainty and over-confidence, instead drawing attention to the mutual vulnerabilities of living in worlds with others and the practice of negotiating and navigating in these shared worlds.

With other feminist scholars, we try to generate affirmative ways of thinking and doing, rather than simply working via critique. We do so by considering multiple perspectives and possibilities, similar to the productive approach described by Donna Haraway: "I also tend to want to work by addition and not by subtraction, multiplying terms to a point where you can foreground them and background them to do different work differently situated" (as cited in Mitman, 2019). Feminist thinking enables us to creatively and expansively remake more-than-human worlds with others. For instance, our intentional engagement with feminist thinking was necessary to challenge the normative nature-culture binaries that are common for understanding gender identity in early childhood education. In previous work, we (Blaise & Rooney, 2020) experiment with a feminist "bringing together method" (p. 156) that encourages open-ended listening and telling practices. We then craft "unruly natureculture gender stories" (p. 155) to illuminate how gender worlds are not exclusively a human process. By attending to the unruly and lively weather relations that are happening with children while walking with weather, we learn how to listen and tell unruly natureculture gender stories that are intentionally situated, embedded and embodied. Cecilia Åsberg, Kathrin Thiele and Iris van der Tuin (2015) remind us of the importance of working with a particular type of feminism that positions flourishing as the central ethical vision. This feminism is "...an embodied, perspectival way of knowing and being in the world...." (Åsberg et al., 2015, p. 151).

In the context of climate change, an increasingly transdisciplinary body of scholarship has continued to emerge between feminism and environmental humanities. This provides space for discussion and collaboration that makes possible new ways of thinking on human-environment relations, along with a myriad of other related fields of research such as extinction studies and discard studies. The environmental humanities scholars that we engage with have a feminist affinity. These scholars think together. There is a criss-crossing of ideas that is constantly generating and building the field in ways that challenge hierarchies and dualist thinking. We briefly expand on this with a few

Young children and environmental education **25**

examples to show how this body of research continues to encourage us to think differently.

Val Plumwood's (1993; 2002) work has been vital for explaining how the knowledge-making that is happening within child-weather relations cannot be grounded in rationalism, possession or mastery to meet the situation of climate change. Plumwood (2002) insists that the environmental problems we are facing will not be addressed by simply accumulating more knowledge or technology. Instead, what is required is the development of "an environmental culture that values and fully acknowledges the non-human sphere and our dependency on it, and is able to make good decisions about how we live and impact on the non-human world" (Plumwood, 2002, p. 3). Plumwood's scholarship is feminist because it considers the multiple ways in which the traditional male-coding of reason still powerfully influences knowledge structures through various subject/object, rational/emotional, mind/body, nature/culture dualisms. Deborah Bird Rose takes up Plumwood's call to simultaneously resituate the animal in the ethical and the human in the ecological throughout her storytelling practices. Rose's feminist sensibility is evident for example through the ways she engages with more-than-human knowledges of flying foxes, flowering gum and Dingoes (Rose, 2011; 2017).

The work of Donna Haraway has shown us new perspectives from which we might question the conceits of human exceptionalism and the foundations of what we think of as knowledge and knowledge-making. For example, Haraway highlights the significance of the situatedness of knowledge and urges us to be wary of the god-tricks of the mind (Haraway, 1988). Haraway also reminds us to be playful with ideas and not to smooth away the difficult things too readily, but rather to "stay with the trouble" of living and dying in these challenging times, so that we might make better worlds together (Haraway, 2016). Both Donna Haraway and Isabelle Stengers remind us that just thinking imaginatively about the future is not enough. Instead, speculation is a methodology or a process that emphasises practice and situatedness (Haraway, 2013). This is feminist because it is not about just thinking in your head, but it is both thinking and doing. This is a feminist act because it attends to the mind/body dualisms not through acts of *either* this *or* that, but always *both and*. By doing *both* thinking *and* doing, speculation becomes a mechanism for everyday knowledge making. It is a bringing together practice.

Isabelle Stengers also teaches us that we need to learn how to occupy the space of *slow science* with practices that are not based on reacting, but instead are responsive. She has also taught us to appreciate "to accept what is messy not as a defect but as what we have to learn to live and think in and with" (Stengers, 2018, p. 12). In the context of climate change, the "slowing down" that Stengers advocates, is not about inaction, but more about making sure that we pause along the way – that we don't rush in ways that are competitive or about gaining control – but rather that we attend to things we might otherwise miss (Stengers, 2013; 2015). In a similar vein, from Anna Tsing, we learn the arts of noticing as we read her ethnography of matsutake mushrooms (Tsing, 2015). She advocates a kind of curiosity and encourages various practices such noticing unruly edges, putting unpredictable encounters at the centre of things, to consider precarity as the condition of our time, and noticing temporalities of the world that are not based on progress. Tsing reminds us that we are surrounded by multiple world-making projects that emerge from practical activities, such as our weather walking. Making worlds is not an exclusively human affair. World making projects can overlap. This overlapping is related to her concept of assemblages (but is different from Gilles Deleuze and Félix Guattari and Bruno Laotour's). Tsing's (2019) variant is a "polyphonic assemblage" (p. 232) which helped her listen to multiple and overlapping worlds differently. A polyphonic assemblage is a shift away from progress rhythms. This reminds us of weather rhythms and how they variously entwine through worlds and times. This body of work also draws attention to the ethical and political aspects of human-environment relations, noting how in a climate change context, such considerations cannot be ignored.

Throughout this book, we draw on these and other scholars (including Thom van Dooren, Elizabeth Povinelli and Kathryn Yusoff) who continue to invite us into generative conversations at the intersection of feminist thinking and environmental humanities.

Conclusion

This book is grounded in a rich history of environmental education and changing ideas about children and childhood(s). We adopt a postdevelopmental approach to early childhood education and speculate on the unique perspective that children might bring to understanding the mutuality and interconnectedness of worldly relations. As a feminist project, we move beyond binary thinking, to consider the situated, responsive, affective and embodied aspects of children's relationships with worlds and learning. To extend our discussion, we also draw on influences from feminist thinking and environmental humanities. We consider differently how children's relations with weather might open possibilities for learning that attend more fully to the complexities of human-weather relations in a climate change era.

Throughout this book, we share some of what we see children doing, thinking or learning, but, just as importantly, we offer a framing that allows us to speculate on what places and other critters might do, think or learn from our mutual presence. We examine experience beyond the human while at the same time acknowledging the human and embodied perspective that we inevitably inhabit (Haraway, 2016). Thus, this is not to impose human agency onto nonhuman bodies or beings, but it is a move towards trying to understand in what sense other places, materials, animals and atmospheres might be interacting, responding or drawing us onwards to ways of knowing worlds that are not just human; brimming with potential that is equally as vital and lively as our own.

References

Ardoin, N., & Bowers, A. (2020). Early childhood environmental education: A systematic review of the research literature. *Educational Research Review, 31*(2020), 1–16. https://doi.org/10.1016/j.edurev.2020.100353

Åsberg, C., Thiele, K., & Van der Tuin, I. (2015). Speculative before the turn: Reintroducing feminist materialist performativity. *Cultural Studies Review, 21*(2), 145–172.

Bawaka Country, Wright, S., Suchet-Pearson, S., & Maymuru, D. (2015). Working with and learning from Country: Decentring human author-ity. *Cultural Geographies, 22*(2), 269–283. https://doi.org/10.1177/1474474014539248

Beery, T., & Jørgensen, K. (2018). Children in nature: Sensory engagement and the experience of biodiversity. *Environmental Education Research, 24*(1), 13–25. https://doi.org/10.1080/13504622.2016.1250149

Blaise, M. (2005). *Playing it straight: Uncovering gender discourse in a kindergarten classroom.* Routledge.

Blaise, M. (2010). New maps for old terrain: Creating a postdevelopmental logic of gender and sexuality in the early years. In L. Brooker & S. Edwards (Eds.), *Engaging play* (pp. 80–95). Open University Press.

Blaise, M., & Rooney, T. (2020). Listening to and telling a rush of Unruly Natureculture gender stories. In F. Nxumalo & C. P. Brown (Eds.), *Disrupting and countering deficits in early childhood education* (pp. 151–163). Routledge.

Bourke, J. (2017). Children's experiences of their everyday walks through a complex urban landscape of belonging. *Children's Geographies, 15*(1), 93–106. https://doi.org/10.1080/14733285.2016.1192582

Campbell, C., & Speldewinde, C. (2020). Affordances for science learning in "Bush kinders". *International Journal of Innovation in Science and Mathematics Education, 28*(3), 1–13.

Ceder, S. (2019). Ice/Water. In P. Rautio & E. Stenvall (Eds.), *Social, material and political constructs of Arctic childhoods-An everyday life perspective* (pp. 35–47). Springer. https://doi.org/10.1007/978-981-13-3161-9

Cutter-Mackenzie, A., Edwards, S., Moore, D., & Boyd, W. (2014). *Young children's play and environmental education in early childhood education.* Springer.

Dahlberg, G., Moss, P., & Pence, A. R. (1999). *Beyond quality in early childhood education and care: Postmodern perspectives.* Psychology Press.

Davis, J. (2009). Revealing the research 'hole' of early childhood education for sustainability: A preliminary survey of the literature. *Environmental Education Research, 15*(2), 227–241. https://doi.org/10.1080/13504620802710607

Davis, J. (Ed.). (2015). *Young children and the environment: Early education for sustainability* (2nd ed.). Cambridge University Press.

Duhn, I., Malone, K., & Tesar, M. (2017). Troubling the intersections of urban/nature/childhood in environmental education. *Environmental Education Research, 23*(10), 1357–1368. https://doi.org/10.1080/13504622.2017.1390884

Edwards, S., & Cutter-Mackenzie, A. (2011). Environmentalising early childhood education curriculum through pedagogies of play. *Australasian Journal of Early Childhood, 36*(1), 51–59. https://doi.org/10.1177/183693911103600109

Elliott, S., Ärlemalm-Hagsér, E., & Davis, J. (2020). *Researching early childhood education for sustainability: Challenging assumptions and orthodoxies* (1st ed.). Routledge. https://doi.org/10.4324/9780429446764

Elliott, S., & Chancellor, B. (2014). From forest preschool to bush kinder: An inspirational approach to preschool provision in Australia. *Australasian Journal of Early Childhood, 39*(4), 45–53. https://doi.org/10.1177%2F183693911403900407

28 A weather learning project

Elliott, S., McCrea, N., Newsome, L., & Gaul, J. (2016). *Examining environmental education in NSW early childhood education services: A literature review with findings from the field.* NSW Environmental Trust. https://www.environment.nsw.gov.au/resources/grants/160418-Early-Childhood-Report.pdf

Flannigan, C., & Dietze, B. (2018). Children, outdoor play, and loose parts. *Journal of Childhood Studies, 42*(4), 53–60. https://doi.org/10.18357/jcs.v42i4.18103

Freeman, C., & Tranter, P. (2011). *Children and their urban environment: Changing worlds* (1st ed.). Routledge. https://doi.org/10.4324/9781849775359

Gill, T. (2007). *No fear: Growing up in a risk averse society.* Calouste Gulbenkian Foundation. https://timrgill.files.wordpress.com/2010/10/no-fear-19-12-07.pdf

Gough, A. (2016). The emergence of environmental education: A 'history' of the field. In R. B. Stevenson, J. D. Brody, & A. Wals (Eds.), *International handbook of research on environmental education* (pp. 13–22). Routledge.

Grogan, L., & Hughes, F. (2020). Pedagogies for ECEfS in Bush Kinder contexts: A comparative report on two Australian studies. In S. Elliott, E. Ärlemalm-Hagsér, & J. Davis (Eds.), *Researching early childhood education for sustainability: Challenging assumptions and orthodoxies* (1st ed., pp. 138–149). Routledge.

Güler Yıldız, T., Öztürk, N., İlhan İyi, T., Aşkar, N., Banko Bal, Ç, Karabekmez, S., & Höl, Ş (2021). Education for sustainability in early childhood education: A systematic review. *Environmental Education Research, 27*(6), 796–820. https://doi.org/10.1080/13504622.2021.1896680

Haraway, D. (1988). Situated knowledges: The science question in feminism and the privilege of partial perspective. *Feminist Studies, 14*(3), 575–599. https://doi.org/10.2307/3178066

Haraway, D. (2013). SF: Science fiction, speculative fabulation, string figures, so far. *Ada: A Journal of Gender, New Media, and Technology, 11*(3), 1–18. http://doi.org/10.7264/N3KH0K81

Haraway, D. (2016). *Staying with the trouble: Making kin in the Chthulucene.* Duke University Press.

Hedefalk, M., Almqvist, J., & Östman, L. (2015). Education for sustainable development in early childhood education: A review of the research literature. *Environmental Education Research, 21*(7), 975–990. https://doi.org/10.1080/13504622.2014.971716

Hickey, A., & Phillips, L. (2013). New kids on the block: Young people, the city and public pedagogies. *Global Studies of Childhood, 3*(2), 115–128. https://doi.org/10.2304/gsch.2013.3.2.115

Horton, J., Christensen, P., Kraftl, P., & Hadfield-Hill, S. (2014). 'Walking… just walking': How children and young people's everyday pedestrian practices matter. *Social & Cultural Geography, 15*(1), 94–115. https://doi.org/10.1080/14649365.2013.864782

James, A., Jenks, C., & Prout, A. (1998). *Theorizing childhood.* Polity Press.

Jenks, C. (2005). *Childhood* (2nd ed.). Routledge.

Katz, C. (2001). The state goes home: Local hypervigilance and the global retreat from social reproduction. *Social Justice, 28*(3), 47–56.

Kraftl, P. (2020). *After childhood: Re-thinking environment, materiality and media in children's lives.* Routledge. https://doi.org/10.4324/9781315110011

Lee, N. (2001). *Childhood and society: Growing up in an age of uncertainty.* Open University Press.

Lenz Taguchi, H. (2010). *Going beyond the theory/practice divide in early childhood education: Introducing an intra-active pedagogy.* Routledge.

Little, H., Elliott, S., & Wyver, S. (Eds.). (2017). *Outdoor learning environments: Spaces for exploration, discovery and risk-taking in the early years.* Allen & Unwin.

Louv, R. (2005). *The last child in the woods: Saving our children from nature-deficit disorder.* Algonquin Books.

MacLeavy, J., Fannin, M., & Larner, W. (2021). Feminism and futurity: Geographies of resistance, resilience and reworking. *Progress in Human Geography, 45*(6), 1558–1579. https://doi.org/10.1177/03091325211003327

Malone, K., & Rudner, J. (2011). Global perspectives on children's independent mobility: A socio-cultural comparison and theoretical discussion of children's lives in four countries in Asia and Africa. *Global Studies of Childhood, 1*(3), 243–259. https://doi.org/10.2304%2Fgsch.2011.1.3.243

Merewether, J. (2015). Young children's perspectives of outdoor learning spaces: What matters? *Australasian Journal of Early Childhood, 40*(1), 99–108. https://doi.org/10.1177/183693911504000113

Mitman, G. (2019). *Reflections on the plantationocene: A conversation with Donna Haraway and Anna Tsing* [Audio Podcast]. Edge Effects. https://edgeeffects.net/haraway-tsing-plantationocene/

Monroe, M. C., Plate, R. R., Oxarart, A., Bowers, A., & Chaves, W. A. (2019). Identifying effective climate change education strategies: A systematic review of the research. *Environmental Education Research, 25*(6), 791–812. https://doi.org/10.1080/13504622.2017.1360842

Mycock, K. (2020). Forest schools: Moving towards an alternative pedagogical response to the Anthropocene? *Discourse: Studies in the Cultural Politics of Education, 41*(3), 427–440. https://doi.org/10.1080/01596306.2019.1670446

Nxumalo, F. (2019). *Decolonizing place in early childhood education.* Routledge.

Pacini-Ketchabaw, V., Kind, S., & Kocher, L. (2016a). *Encounters with materials in early childhood education.* Routledge.

Pacini-Ketchabaw, V., Taylor, A., & Blaise, M. (2016b). Decentring the human in multispecies ethnographies. In C. A. Taylor & C. Hughes (Eds.), *Posthuman research practices in education* (pp. 149–167). Palgrave Macmillan

Plumwood, V. (1993). *Feminism and the mastery of nature.* Routledge.

Plumwood, V. (2002). *Environmental culture: The ecological crisis of reason.* Routledge.

Prout, A. (2005). *The future of childhood: Towards the interdisciplinary study of children.* Routledge.

Rinaldi, C. (2006). *In dialogue with Reggio Emilia: Listening, researching and learning.* Routledge.

Rooney, T. (2015). Higher stakes – The hidden risks of school security fences for children's learning environments, *Environmental Education Research, 21*(6), 885–898. https://doi.org/10.1080/13504622.2014.936308

Rose, D. B. (2011). *Wild dog dreaming: Love and extinction.* University of Virginia Press.

Rose, D. B. (2017). Shimmer: When all you love is being trashed. In A. Tsing, H. Swanson, E. Gan, & N. Bubandt (Eds), *Arts of living on a damaged planet* (pp. G51–G63). University of Minnesota Press.

Rousell, D., & Cutter-Mackenzie-Knowles, A. (2020). A systematic review of climate change education: Giving children and young people a 'voice' and a 'hand' in redressing climate change. *Children's Geographies, 18*(2), 191–208. https://doi.org/10.1080/14733285.2019.1614532

Sandseter, E. B. H. (2009). Affordances for risky play in preschool: The importance of features in the play environment. *Early Childhood Education Journal, 36*(5), 439–446. https://doi.org/10.1007/s10643-009-0307-2

Sandseter, E. B. H. (2014). Early childhood education and care practitioners' perceptions of children's risky play; Examining the influence of personality and gender. *Early Child Development and Care, 184*(3), 434–449. https://doi.org/10.1080/03004430.2013.794797

Sandseter, E. B. H., & Hagen, T. L. (2016). Scandinavian early childhood education: Spending time in the outdoors. In B. Humberstone, H. Prince, & K. A. Henderson (Eds.), *Routledge international handbook of outdoor studies* (pp. 95–102). Taylor & Francis Group.

Sharma-Brymer, V., & Bland, D. (2016). Bringing nature to schools to promote children's physical activity. *Sports Medicine*, *46*(7), 955–962. https://doi.org/10.1007/s40279-016-0487-z

Somerville, M. (2017). The Anthropocene's call to educational research. In K. Malone, T. Gray, & S. Truong (Eds.), *Reimagining sustainability in precarious times* (pp. 17–28). Springer.

Somerville, M., & Williams, C. (2015). Sustainability education in early childhood: An updated review of research in the field. *Contemporary Issues in Early Childhood*, *16*(2), 102–117.

Stengers, I. (2013). Matters of Cosmopolitics: On the provocations of Gaia. Isabelle Stengers in conversation with Heather Davis and Etienne Turpin. In E. Turpin (Ed.), *Architecture in the Anthropocene. Encounters among design, deep time, science and philosophy* (pp. 171–182). Open Humanities Press.

Stengers, I. (2015). *In catastrophic times: Resisting the coming barbarism*. Open Humanities Press.

Stengers, I. (2018). *Another science is possible: A manifesto for slow science*. Wiley

Taylor, A. (2013). *Reconfiguring the natures of childhood*. Routledge.

Taylor, A. (2017). Romancing or reconfiguring nature? Towards common worlds pedagogies. In K. Malone, S. Truong, & T. Gray (Eds.), *Reimagining sustainability education in precarious times* (pp. 61–75). Springer.

Taylor, A., & Pacini-Ketchabaw, V. (2015). Learning with children, ants, and worms in the Anthropocene: Towards a common world pedagogy of multispecies vulnerability. *Pedagogy, Culture & Society*, *23*(4), 507–529. https://doi.org/10.1080/14681366.2015.1039050

Tsing, A. L. (2015). *The mushroom at the end of the world: On the possibility of life in capitalist ruins*. Princeton University Press.

Tsing, A. L. (2019). When the things we study respond to each other: Tools for unpacking "the material". In P. Harvey, C. Krohn-Hansen, & K. G. Nustad (Eds.), *Anthropos and the material* (pp. 221–243). Duke University Press. https://www.dukeupress.edu/anthropos-and-the-material

Valentine, G. (2004). *Public space and the culture of childhood*. Ashgate.

Valentine, G., & McKendrick, V. (1997). Children's outdoor play: Exploring parental concerns about children's safety and the changing nature of childhood. *Geoforum*, *28*(2), 219–235. https://doi.org/10.1016/S0016-7185(97)00010-9

Verlie, B., & Flynn, A. (2022). School strike for climate: A reckoning for education. *Australian Journal of Environmental Education*, *38*(1), 1–12. https://doi.org/10.1017/aee.2022.5

Yelland, N. (2007). *Shift to the future: Rethinking learning with new technologies in education*. Routledge.

PART II

Methods: Thinking, moving and writing with weather

3
THINKING WITH WEATHER

In the presence of the sculpture "Ngaraka: Shrine for the lost Koori" (Mundine &
Foley, 2001) we remember that while we only pass through this place briefly, the
process of weathering continues unabated. The rusty red steel frame and bleached
kangaroo bones beneath attest to the weathering wrought by sun, rain, wind and
cold. Yet, this is not only the "weathering" of erosion, corrosion and decay, but
"weathering" as resilience and a lively continuing of peoples, stories, memories and
materials that linger and move through this place along with the ever-changing ele-
mental conditions.

(Taylor & Rooney, 2016a)

Introduction

In some respects, contemporary Western understandings of weather are both
sophisticated and complex. The rise of mobile devices and human interest in
everyday weather has spawned the development of weather apps that are the go-to
source of information on rain, humidity, UV index and much more. Similarly,
the impact of human activity on the climate has (albeit long overdue) found its
way into public debate, and with this has come a growing acknowledgement of
the connection between changing climate patterns and extreme weather events
such as floods, drought or hurricanes. While knowledge of weather and climate
continues to grow, there is a sense in which weather is still seen as separate or
out there (Ingold, 2015; Vannini et al., 2012); something we can lock ourselves
away from, adapt to or build up barriers as protection against more extreme
conditions. In this regard, the ways we think about and with weather remain
somewhat centred on our everyday (human) activities and need for comfort and
safety, with less consideration given to other notions of weather or weathering
that are not captured in an app or in daily weather reports. One aim in this book

DOI: 10.4324/9781003150411-5

34 Methods: Thinking, moving and writing with weather

is to broaden ways of thinking about and with weather to encompass more-than-human relations and considerations.

In this chapter, we share the conceptual influences that continue to shape our practices of thinking with weather. We first explain key ideas from recent research that have challenged us to attend to human-weather relations differently; ideas such as weather worlds, weather bodies, weather place-making and weathering. In the second half of this chapter, we turn to Indigenous knowledges of weather and climate, including insights from the book *Song Spirals* by the Gay'wu group of women, which invites us to further consider human relations with weather, seasons and more-than-human worlds through Indigenous perspectives (Burarrwanga et al., 2019). We acknowledge there are many layers to Indigenous wisdom and reading *Song Spirals* has been an opportunity to listen to the knowledge that is shared. We conclude this chapter with some reflections on what it means to think with weather and recognise that we are not so much offering a discovery of anything new, but rather sharing an attempt to seek out ways of knowing that have been carried within Earth, weathers and peoples for many thousands of years. We think with weather knowledges across time, space and culture to better understand the potential of thinking with weather for environmental education practice.

Weather worlds

Scientific research on climate change and weather helps us to understand the atmospheric, geological, biological and meteorological dimensions of climate change. This book is neither outside nor inside science but offers a way of thinking with weather that aims to complement and extend science thinking and learning in education contexts. When we talk of science, we do not limit this to Western and non-Indigenous approaches to science but extend this to sciences that some recognise as specifically Indigenous sciences (Liboiron, 2021). We understand science, along with the humanities, education and other disciplines, as coming together in the making of and responding to new climate worlds. Therefore, we do not distinguish between scientific and non-scientific weather learning in our approach to environmental education. Instead, our interest is in extending practices of *learning about weather* (which tends to be the traditional mode of teaching the science of weather or climate change in classroom contexts) to *learning with weather* (as what we hope to add as we look to the potential of embodied and place-based knowledges, the arts and speculative thinking). We take this further still, by recognising that we can think of humans as not just entangled with weather, but in many ways *as weather*; a notion that opens possibilities for how we might integrate weather into children's environmental learning through what we refer to as weather learning.

It seems obvious to say that we can only really come to know weather by being out and about in rain, sunshine, wind or snow. As Tim Ingold (2010) notes, there is an "intimate relation between becoming knowledgeable, walking along and the experience of weather" (p. 121). We come to know the smells and feel of the elements, the memories they evoke, the comforts and discomforts of certain conditions and the daily clothing decisions that weather demands of us. However, there is more to our human weather experience than being *in* weather. Weather is not simply an external atmosphere that surrounds our presence, but something more deeply entangled with our lives and bodies. In reflecting on the relationship between weather, land and air, Ingold (2007) argues:

> *fundamental to life is the process of respiration, by which organisms continually disrupt any boundary between earth and sky .... Thus to inhabit the open is not to be stranded on the outer surface of the earth but to be caught up in the transformations of the weather-world.*
>
> *(p. 19)*

Ingold's notion of the weather-world provides a starting point for thinking about how (as humans) we live with weather and what it might mean to understand humans, weather and other bodies and beings as mutually shaping shared weather worlds. The act of breathing is itself a transformative exchange and an entanglement of humans, atmosphere and weather.

In contrast to Ingold's *world*, we draw insight from John Law (2015) preferring the plural *worlds* to encompass not only the potential worlds across time and space but also the co-existent multiple life worlds of other creatures and matters. We cannot hold all of these in a singular notion *world*. Further, thinking with worlds, allows us to explore what it means to make different worlds with weather.

Astrida Neimanis and Rachel Walker (2014) also explain the significance of thinking about the relationship between humans and weather as inseparable: "the weather and the climate are not phenomena 'in' which we live at all – where climate would be some natural backdrop to our separate human dramas – but are rather of us, in us, through us" (Neimanis & Walker, 2014, p. 559). This framing of humans and weather as non-discrete entities helps to disrupt our human-centric tendency to view Earth as something available for us to *do things to* and weather as something that *happens to us*. These ideas hold significance for environmental education as they impact on how we position ourselves in relation to what we are teaching and learning.

Weather bodies

One consistent theme in recent writing on weather, is the idea that – as soon as we attune to weather in our lives – it makes no sense to talk of our bodies as somehow separate from Earth. As Tim Edensor (2021) remarks, "immersed in realms of light, weather and earthliness, any sense that we are embodied human entities separated from the landscape is deceptive" (p. 147).

In Edensor's (2021) reflection on what it means to weather through light, he describes the sensory experience of light in different locations across the globe. He acknowledges the shortcoming of our human visual capabilities but draws attention to the way light features in our encounters that we might sometimes take for granted: "the qualities of tone, intensity, reflection, colour and shadow that [sunlight] bestows upon place are integral to everyday experience" (Edensor, 2021, p. 157). Light and shadow play a prominent part in our observations of children walking with weather, offering another perspective on how we might understand weather and worlds, as in the following small story from one of our walks.

> *A child laughs, watching a shadow follow her along. It can be hard to escape a shadow. Another child sees her shadow disappear without warning. Lost, never to appear in the same form again. Small everyday moments are mingled with wider planetary movements of sun and Earth. With shadows, perhaps children also sense the fleetingness of their own presence, or in some small way are seeking out connections across deeper times and places. Shadows reveal multiple weather connections between light, heat, intensity and moving bodies of child, earth and sun.*
>
> *(Adapted from Rooney, 2019)*

In such encounters, children seem to recognise shadows as a phenomenon that is both in and out of their control. They enjoy a playful exchange with shifts in light, position, time, place and moving bodies (see Figure 3.1). Shadows shift and shape too along with the movements of other weather bodies.

FIGURE 3.1 Walking with shadows

Weather can thus be understood as so entangled with bodies and everyday lives that it is impossible to draw a boundary between body and weather. Humans absorb, release, inhale or exhale air, wind, sun and moisture from both sky and Earth: "to feel the wind is not to make external, tactile contact with our surroundings but to mingle with them" (Ingold, 2007, p. 19). As we breathe in air or draw heat from the sun, we notice the porosity of our bodies (Neimanis & Walker, 2014). The sensory and affective ways we come to know weather are significant; yet at the same time, this is much more than a physical exchange of energy and matter. Human relations with weather can also be understood as co-constitutive of worlds and meaning. There is "… an intimate knowing. A weather-beaten face is one that is enfolded and inscribed by life and the weather – it is weathered" (Adams-Hutcheson, 2021, p. 223). In this intimacy, we recognise that connections to weather far exceed a singular encounter and that our bodies hold traces of what it means to live with weather.

These minglings of body and weather invite us to think of human bodies as weather bodies. The notion of weather bodies describes the transcorporeality (Alaimo, 2010) or movement between human and weather such that neither is discrete or separable. That is, "the ebb and flow of meteorological life transits through us, just as the actions, matters and meanings of our own bodies return to the climate in a myriad of ways" (Neimanis & Walker, 2014, p. 560). Neimanis and Walker (2014) see this as a way of attuning ourselves to the world; "as weather bodies, mutually caught up in the whirlwind of a weather-world" (p. 562). We take from this the idea that if humans become more attuned to the weather in and of our bodies, then we might also develop a stronger sensibility towards the part humans play in the weathering of worlds. We come to see our (human) selves as making meaning and worlds with weather, and the responsibility this entails.

In our work, we imagine human bodies as weather bodies, and extend this thinking such that "all bodies including human, earth, water, animal and plant bodies, are weather bodies" (Pollitt et al., 2021, p. 2). Encounters with trees featured strongly on our walks with children (see Figure 3.2), not just as an indicator of seasonal change, but as weathered and weathering bodies that invite ways of being together with weather.

A pale Eucalyptus tree glows in the sunlight. Its dark grey bark has shed and lies in shreds at its base. The bark is flexible but not yet brittle enough to be crunchy underfoot. A child reaches to touch the bare trunk, getting a feel for its new smooth texture. Other children gather strands of bark and lean them against the trunk alongside those still hanging from the tree. Low broad branches of other nearby trees prove irresistible for children who like to climb. They find perches in the boughs, rest their back against its coarse trunk, and wrap their bodies around its solid limbs. Bodies. Sheltering. Weather bodies, weathered bodies, weathering together.

(Adapted from Taylor & Rooney, 2016b)

38 Methods: Thinking, moving and writing with weather

FIGURE 3.2 Falling bark shelter

Thinking of all bodies as weather bodies draws attention to the shifts and seasonality in life, movement, matter and decay. Thinking with weather bodies helps us attune to the inseparability of body and weather, as well as the ways that human and more-than-humans are entangled with weather.

Weather place-making

Place and place relations also feature strongly in research on human-weather relations. In the work of Phillip Vannini et al. (2012), for example, we are reminded of the relationship between weather and place-making, such that we can never think of place without weather, and the changes we witness come about because "weather constantly makes and remakes place" (p. 364). To think of the place-making actions of weather, is to be reminded of the ways rain, wind and sunshine shape the contours and meanings of place. Yet, we can also think of the mutual shaping between weather and place as a form of weather-place making. Place is more than the surfaces we walk across, more than the array of materials, buildings and landmarks that lie across a landscape. Iris Duhn (2017) describes place as a site of vital materialities and intensities and a co-constitution between entities and forces. Weathering forces are thus all at once a mix of materiality, movement and making with place. Water and wind move Earth and matter, shifting the terrain and the paths and movements of other materials and bodies. Weather is making place and place makes weather.

As humans, our experience of place is deeply connected to weather. Some have observed, for example, "[f]ew of our mundane activities remain untouched by weather" (Vannini et al., 2012, p. 377) and "weather mobilises us to feel a connection to places and times, to remember seasons past and to feel the delicious anticipation of future weather" (Adams-Hutcheson, 2021, p. 222). Vannini et al. (2012) draw attention to the co-constitution of humans, place and weather, noting that "weathering is an embodied practice, a performance through which we transform the weather-places in which we dwell, and the individuals that we are" (p. 377). As humans, we are constantly reminded of the relationship between weather and movement. Our day-to-day experience brings awareness of the "impermanence, transience, instability, evanescence, and uncertainty of weather" (Vannini et al., p. 374). While the work of Vannini et al. (2012) focuses on human experience of weather, it provides useful insights into the ways that all kinds of bodies and places are transformed by and transform weather.

In our work with children, even the smallest of encounters remind us of the many ways Earth is weathered by and weathers our presence; for example, soil is compacted by footprints and stones by the lake seem to invite children to fling them into the water. We are led to reflect on Doreen Massey's (2005) suggestion to think of spaces as lively where a negotiation must take place "within and between both human and non-human" (p. 140). Our human presence in place is a negotiation; a way of moving where humans are part of the shifting and shaping of the places themselves.

Weathering together

Another key theme is the idea that weather is not just a thing, but a process. Hence, we can talk of Earth as weathering both the elements and our presence, and we can talk of weather bodies weathering each other. Weathering reminds us of enduring tough times and resilience. There is also a sense of mutual vulnerability. While humans are vulnerable to raging fires, floods and storms, our human activity in turn makes Earth systems vulnerable to rising temperatures and sea levels. The notion of weathering allows us to envisage human relations with weather, climate and place, as the ongoing and always moving multitude of more-than-human species and inhabitants who are *weathering together* these chaotic times.

Weathering together is to both be vulnerable and to make others vulnerable. Yet, while it is easy to think of vulnerability as something negative and to be avoided, there is another way in which we can understand its potential. Rosi Braidotti (2013), in writing on wider relations of mutual interdependence, suggests that we can look at human interaction with others without having to see this through "the reactive bond of vulnerability" (p. 50). Braidotti looks to a more "affirmative bond that locates the subject in the flow of relations with multiple others" (p. 50). That is, Braidotti suggests we need to move beyond

40 Methods: Thinking, moving and writing with weather

seeing our interconnectedness to others (human and nonhuman) as a kind of necessary bond in the face of larger common threats such as climate change, and instead look to the vital potential in these relations. It is this vital potentiality that is a feminist move towards worldings or worlding well together because it is affirmative and productive. To acknowledge the mutual vulnerability in the weather relations between humans and more-than-human worlds, as we have above, is therefore not to suggest this is a reactive or negative state of affairs that we have to accept and live with. Such a position would lead to despondence and inertia. Rather, it is to recognise that in vulnerability, there is a vital and generative potential. Weather forces can swirl, destroy, surprise or bring to life. If humans can accept the responsibility and risk that mutual vulnerabilities give rise to (Hird, 2013; Taylor & Pacini-Ketchabaw, 2015), rather than focus efforts on futile attempts to eradicate vulnerability, then perhaps we can remain open to ways of living well with others in changing weather worlds. This is a theme we expand on in later chapters.

On hot summer days, during our walks, busy ant's nests often drew the children's attention. If children walked over a nest without thinking, they soon became aware of the ants underfoot, and would leap sideways – wondering whether they had trod on any ants while at the same time shaking their feet and legs to avoid being bitten. Ant-child relations – particularly in the heat of the midday sun or with the smell of an approaching storm – can be flurried, and yet also filled with the children's recognition of the strength and vulnerability of these small critters. Affrica Taylor and Veronica Pacini-Ketchabaw (2015), take this recognition a step further, saying that in encounters with ants and worms:

> (w)e might reduce our conceited sense of human exceptionalism with the humbling recognition that the daily work of worms and ants provides the conditions of possibility for much life on earth, including ours. The knowledge, of course, also matters in our pedagogies.
>
> (p. 515)

This mutual weathering between ants, earth and humans exhibits both vulnerability and the ongoingness of relations that shift and shape new weather worlds. Weathering is thus more than a geological process, and it is more than a sense of holding strong in the face of opposing forces. It involves both of these and more. Weathering builds, erodes and shapes worlds. Neimanis and Walker (2014) draw on the work of Karen Barad to explain this further: "Barad's understanding of things as perpetually worlding – that is, as materializing from the intra-actions of always emergent things-in-phenomena – suggests to us the concept of weathering" (p. 561).

Weathering, more specifically *weathering together*, is a collective endeavour where to weather is to both resist and generate new climate worlds. It is a form of weather worlding where "human, non-human and elemental conditions are entangled in a collective world-making" (Rooney, 2018, p. 2). In weather worlds,

Thinking with weather **41**

we can therefore understand humans as both co-implicated and co-makers with weather and other weather bodies (Ingold, 2015; Neimanis & Walker, 2014).

Indigenous weather knowledges

There are deeper weather knowledges and cultures that speak to an entwined view of human relations with Earth and weather, and that also draw attention to the limitations of thinking that humans can somehow separate themselves from weather or weather events. In Australia, Indigenous peoples have nurtured relations with place and weather for many thousands of years, living or co-becoming with Country:

> *Country is home and land, but it is more than that. It is the seas and the waters, the rocks and the soils, the animals and winds and people too. It is the connections between those beings, and their dreams and emotions, their languages and their Law. Country is the way humans and non-humans co-become, the way we emerge together, have always emerged together and will always emerge together.*
>
> *(Burarrwanga et al., 2019, p. xxii)*

This extract from *Song spirals* revealed to us the deeper stories and songs of Indigenous Australians, making it possible to sense some of the ways in which everything is interconnected: "We come from our place and we make our place and we are our place" (Burarrwanga et al., 2019, p. 23).

In colonial contexts such as Australia, Sarah Wright et al. (2021) remind us that place has been "weathered in deeply racist, entitled and possessive ways across time and space" (p. 207). Indigenous peoples have had to weather "the damage of ongoing colonisation" and yet at the same time persist and weather this destruction by "continuing to know and live with weather in diverse and place-based ways" (p. 207). This raises an important insight; that is, weather (along with people and land) is bound up in colonisation practices, and Indigenous peoples have had to resist the ongoing erasure of weather cultures along with all other manners of invasion. Wright et al. (2021) draw attention to the ways in which, in 1901 the selection of the site on which Canberra would be built as the capital Australia, was an act of colonial privilege that was deeply entangled with weather. The decision was based in part on the cold climate that was said to suit the processes of governing for white, male invaders from the United Kingdom (Wright et al., 2021), while Indigenous connections to Country and weather were ignored and rendered invisible. A similar observation has been made in New Zealand where "if colonisation meant taking land for the settler project, it also involved promoting scientific weather knowledge and often erased alternatives" (Adams-Hutcheson, 2021, p. 226). Māori hold a deep understanding of weather and climate, yet this has been overridden or ignored by settlers. As Gail Adams-Hutcheson (2021) notes, "colonial weather and climate knowledge have had an essential and fundamentally practical purpose – to ensure settler's success"

42 Methods: Thinking, moving and writing with weather

(p. 226). For our own research, conducted on the land now known as Canberra, Australia, the notion that the weathers we walked with also carried the scars of colonisation along with people and land, was a sobering insight. We have since come to understand that colonial legacies shape not just knowledge, but also the way we live with weather and climate, and this requires more attention.

Wright et al. (2021) also point out however that, just as the practices of colonisation are ongoing, so too are the processes of weathering and that "in spite of efforts to order and contain, weather is unruly, evading regimes of colonial control" (pp. 214–215). Perhaps then, when we attempt to think with weather as uncontained and we practice ways of noticing human becomings with weather, we might be prying open ways of knowing weather that help to challenge the colonial assumptions inevitably embedded in non-Indigenous understandings of weather.

Thus, as we think with weather, we acknowledge and respect the deeper weather knowledges that persist despite the powers of colonisation that have sought to erase Indigenous culture and connections to Country. We continue to listen, understand and learn of new ways to think with weather and weather worlds. This is another example of how, to weather is not only to suffer damaging contexts and conditions, but it is also to persist and live with conditions that make and shape complex life worlds. As non-Indigenous peoples, it seems that it is only when confronted with obvious human-driven impacts of climate change that perhaps we can finally begin to recognise something we should always have known, that "[t]he beings and becomings of weather must be lived with in order to co-exist" (Wright et al., 2021, pp. 214–215), and that how we live with weather matters.

The small story at the beginning of this chapter tells of an encounter with the *Ngaraka: Shrine for the lost Koori*; a sculpture created by two Aboriginal artists (Djon Mundine and Fiona Foley) that sits in the landscape where we walked with children. The sculpture is made of kangaroo bones, paper bark and steel tubing, and evokes histories of weathering, resilience, death, life, becoming and stories told through wind, sun, earth and rain. On our walks with children, we would often stop at *Ngaraka* (see Figure 3.3). Children would stand or sit with the bones, or tap the bones against the steel poles, listening and evoking resonant tubular tunes. We would talk and remember the Indigenous people who have been living on and with this land for many thousands of years; long before Canberra was built or its central lake, Lake Burley Griffin, was even conceived or constructed.

Over time, we returned on many walks to *Ngaraka*, and witnessed the weathering of kangaroo bones as they softened and became tinged with a mossy green. Small spiders inhabited the hollow bones. At times children would try to reconstruct what they imagined a kangaroo might look like; often comparing the weathered bones to those in their own bodies. On one of our last visits, some children began to make mini shrine sculptures from the bones. We often stayed with *Ngaraka* for a while, and then moved on, attuning more closely to the tensions between the sculpture as a powerful reminder of the resilience of First Nations cultures and the surrounding landscape scarred with evidence of ongoing colonisation practices. The sculpture, combined with practices of returning and remembering, prompted us to keep pondering the implications of our own

Thinking with weather 43

FIGURE 3.3 *Ngaraka: Shrine for the lost Koori* with rain and child

entanglement in the colonial and ecological inheritances of the place (Taylor & Rooney, 2016c).

In the book *Song Spirals*, we are drawn into a world of stories and singing where "the patterns and connections of weather are fore-grounded" (Bawaka Country et al., 2020, p. 301). As we read, we are excited and hopeful. Here is a chance to listen and reflect further on the small insights we have gleaned from trying to notice the entanglements of place and weather with children. We wonder how in reading and listening we might think differently. There are many stories in *Song Spirals* that draw us into different ways of considering time, place, people and weather. As readers, we are offered the following invitation:

> We want you to touch, and hear, our world. Because when children are little they learn from touching, feeling, doing. But when we talk, talk, talk, they don't learn. We invite you to sit on the ground with us. We can balance both cultures, we can share. We will treat you as family.
>
> (Burarrwanga et al., 2019, p. xxvi)

44 Methods: Thinking, moving and writing with weather

As a result, we sit on the ground and listen. As we do so, we soon realise we are not just listening to story and song but are learning how to listen to and with clouds and wind.

Clouds

We hear the liveliness of Country. We recognise that clouds and Country are not just about what we, adults and children, might say or see. Clouds have things to see and say too.

> *Our sound goes to the clouds as we walk to our homeland. The clouds collect the sound, and later it will rain. … Now we are walking, our sound, our existence, everything comes to life; the laughter and joy of being home, coming home, it weaves up into the air, to the clouds.*
>
> *(Burarrwanga et al., 2019, p. 85)*

We hear of how the clouds give messages to each other. They are communicating. And we hear that to listen to clouds is to learn.

> *The clouds say, 'I am now passing this place, I am now passing this place', all Dhuwa places. The clouds are saying this. They are stopping at one place, then the next. They are gathering. … We are all on a journey together. We are the clouds. … The clouds know things too, and they talk.*
>
> *(Burarrwanga et al., 2019, p. 105; 108)*

We have looked up at clouds so many times with children on our walks. Pointing out shifting creatures in the forms of the clouds or tracing the contrails of a plane overhead. We had not however stopped to listen to clouds. What might we have heard, we wonder, if we had attended differently to stories being told through the lively movement of clouds?

Wind

The wind communicates too and has things to say.

> *The wind does not just blow. It communicates, it tells us things, it has its own story and Law, its own ceremony. The wind is its being and its becoming. It co-becomes with us and with Country.*
>
> *(Burarrwanga et al., 2019, p. 20)*

Through these words, we are challenged to consider wind in a radically different way. On our walks with children, we have often felt wind and how wind blows. We notice leaves and creatures responding to wind and sense the wind as it moves our bodies along. Children try to hold hats tight on their heads, but when they move with wind, hats fly off into the air (see Figure 3.4).

Thinking with weather 45

FIGURE 3.4 "Hold on to your hat"

Yet, reading *Song Spirals* shows us how much we may have missed. We wonder, have we really listened to wind? Or have we focused too much on watching the children? And if we could listen differently to wind, what stories might we hear? What stories are being told when wind rushes through trees and leaves rustle? There is so much more for us to explore in understanding how wind and children become with each other, and more in understanding what it might mean to learn with wind and to notice learning beyond the perspective of the child. Together with the non-Indigenous members of the Bawaka collective, we too experience this as "a steep learning curve" as we try to become "less hard-of-hearing in the context of a communicative and vibrant more-than-human-world" (Bawaka Country et al., 2015, p. 278).

From *Song Spirals*, singing and storying become for us new ways of knowing language and land, and while we can listen only on the surface, there is a resonance and pull towards something in Earth out of reach but knowing that it is there. The Gay'wu group of women tell their stories so that non-Indigenous

46 Methods: Thinking, moving and writing with weather

peoples can begin to understand the relationship between people and Country and singing. The women remind us that: "Living our responsibilities means opening ourselves up to being surprised and transformed, to changing what we do and to trying to do things that make a positive difference" (Burarrwanga et al., 2019, p. 105). We do not know how we might redress some of the human damage that continues to be done to Earth, but perhaps this is looking too far ahead. Instead, we continue from where we have started – with a desire to attend better to human relations with land, weather and more-than-human worlds – to see what unfolds and to understand this more deeply through the ways of weather.

Conclusion

Thinking with children and weather draws us into new ways of noticing our surrounds and the critters and things that share the world. Listening to stories of Bawaka Country pulls us towards something that makes us rethink our place and connection with worlds that we have come to consider as weather worlds. In the larger scheme of weather and worlds, our thinking is far from new. Rather, it is more a recognition that there seems to be much missing from learning about weather in current education contexts, as we remind ourselves that "[t]here is nothing new about attending to weather for the many Indigenous lifeworlds that have engaged the beings, co-becomings and agencies of weather for millennia" (Wright et al., 2021, p. 208).

What remains new for us, is recognising the ongoing possibilities for shaping worlds between people, climate, land and creatures in ways that might be responsive and recuperative in light of current climate challenges. What matters is that we do not only look forward, but that we sometimes return, reflect and look differently on practices and frameworks that we so often take for granted in education, including the knowledge systems that come to dominate thinking at the expense of others. In our practice, we have noticed a lively vibrancy in the relations between children and the educators who encourage the children's curiosity, in ways that suggest an openness to learning with the possibilities of place and weather. Our hope is that walking and learning with weather offers a perspective that reminds us to look beyond our human concerns, and to better understand what it means to live with and listen to the weathers that shape our shared climate worlds.

Understanding our human relationship to the weather differently, helps us to envisage the potential of working with human–weather relations as a mode of learning with the environment that fosters connection to climatic activity. Neimanis and Walker (2014) invite us to "reimagine our bodies as archives of climate change and as making future climate possible" (p. 558). As young children explore or respond to fleeting lines of feeling, thought or action within their day-to-day weather encounters, they generate new ways of becoming with climate worlds.

In this chapter we have considered diverse ways of thinking with and knowing weather, weaving together the research, stories and songs that continue to influence our thinking and practice. Alongside meteorology and climate and earth sciences, children can also learn with weather in ways that invoke more deeply other lives and histories in coming to know a weathered and weathering world. Our approach to thinking with weather is difficult to distinguish from the *doing* aspects of our research. In the next two chapters we turn specifically to our practices of walking with weather and writing with weather. Taken together, thinking, walking and writing, are three entwined dimensions of our method and pedagogical practice. This does not seek to replace conventional approaches to education research and practice, but rather, with Pauliina Rautio (2021), it aims to draw attention to "alternative ways of knowing" (p. 2) and to increase the richness of the ways we understand and do things through our research. For Rautio, post-qualitative research brings an invitation to map relations and intersectional entanglements that in turn provide a basis for alternative stories, and these "new stories might bring needed transformations in the world" (Rautio, 2021, p. 3). We place an emphasis on human–weather entanglements so that we too might tell new stories of relations with the more-than-human world (or notice stories that the children might tell) in the hope that this might add to how we come to know the implications of weather within worlds we inhabit.

References

Adams-Hutcheson, G. (2021). Dwelling and weather: Farming in a mobilised climate. In K. Barry, M. Borovnik & T. Edensor (Eds.), *Weather: Spaces, mobilities and affects* (pp. 222–235). Routledge.

Alaimo, S. (2010). *Bodily natures: Science, environment and the material self.* Indiana University Press.

Bawaka Country, Wright, S., Suchet-Pearson, S., & Maymuru, D. (2015). Working with and learning from Country: Decentring human author-ity. *Cultural Geographies, 22*(2), 269–283. https://doi.org/10.1177/1474474014539248

Bawaka Country, Wright, S., Suchet-Pearson, S., Lloyd, K., Burarrwanga, L., Ganambarr, R., Ganambarr-Stubbs, M., Ganambarr, B., & Maymuru, D. (2020). Gathering of the clouds: Attending to Indigenous understandings of time and climate through songspirals. *Geoforum, 108*, 295–304. https://doi.org/10.1016/j.geoforum.2019.05.017

Braidotti, R. (2013). *The posthuman*. Polity Press.

Burarrwanga, L., Ganambarr, R., Ganambarr-Stubbs, M., Ganambarr, B., Maymuru, D., Wright, S. L., Suchet-Pearson, S., & Lloyd, K. (2019). *Song spirals: Sharing women's wisdom of Country through songlines*. Allen & Unwin.

Duhn, I. (2017). Cosmopolitics of place: Towards urban multispecies living in precarious times. In M. Malone, S. Truong, & T. Gray (Eds.), *Reimagining sustainability in precarious times* (pp. 45–57). Springer.

Edensor, T. (2021). Seeing with Australian light: Representations and landscapes. In K. Barry, M. Borovnik, & T. Edensor (Eds.), *Weather: Spaces, mobilities and affects* (pp. 145–158). Routledge.

Hird, M. J. (2013). Waste, landfills, and an environmental ethic of vulnerability. *Ethics and the Environment, 18*(1), 105–124. https://doi.org/10.2979/ethicsenviro.18.1.105

48 Methods: Thinking, moving and writing with weather

Ingold, T. (2007). Earth, sky, wind, and weather. *Journal of the Royal Anthropological Institute*, *13*(2007), S19–S38. https://doi.org/10.1111/j.1467-9655.2007.00401.x

Ingold, T. (2010). Footprints through the weather-world: Walking, breathing, knowing. *Journal of the Royal Anthropological Institute*, 16, S121–S139. https://doi.org/10.1111/j.1467-9655.2010.01613.x

Ingold, T. (2015). *The life of lines*. Routledge.

Law, J. (2015). What's wrong with a one-world world? *Distinktion: Scandinavian Journal of Social Theory*, *16*(1), 126–139. https://doi.org/10.1080/1600910X.2015.1020066

Liboiron, M. (2021). *Pollution is colonialism*. Duke University Press.

Massey, D. (2005). *For space*. SAGE.

Mundine, D., & Foley, F. (2001). *Ngaraka: Shrine for the Lost Koori*. Australian National University Art Collection.

Neimanis, A., & Walker, R. L. (2014). Weathering: Climate change and the "thick time" of transcorporeality. *Hypatia*, *29*(3), 558–575.

Pollitt, J., Blaise, M., & Rooney, T. (2021). Weather bodies: Experimenting with dance improvisation in environmental education in the early years. *Environmental Education Research*, *27*(8), 1141–1151. https://doi.org/10.1080/13504622.2021.1926434

Rautio, P. (2021). Post-qualitative inquiry: Four balancing acts in crafting alternative stories to live by. *Qualitative Inquiry*, *27*(2), 228–230. https://doi.org/10.1177/1077800420933297

Rooney, T. (2018). Weather worlding: Learning with the elements in early childhood. *Environmental Education Research*, *24*(1), 1–12. https://doi.org/10.1080/13504622.2016.1217398

Rooney, T. (2019, November 28). With shadows, what connections might be forged beyond here and now?. *Common Worlds Research Collective*. https://commonworlds.net/with-shadows-what-connections-might-be-forged-beyond-here-and-now/

Taylor, A., & Pacini-Ketchabaw, V. (2015). Learning with children, ants, and worms in the Anthropocene: Towards a common world pedagogy of multispecies vulnerability. *Pedagogy, Culture & Society*, *23*(4), 507–529. https://doi.org/10.1080/14681366.2015.1039050

Taylor, A., & Rooney, T. (2016a, March 20). Weathering in wild weather times. *Walking with Wildlife in Wild Weather Times-A Common World Childhoods Research Collective Blog*. https://walkingwildlifewildweather.com/2016/03/20/weathering-in-wild-weather-times/

Taylor, A., & Rooney, T. (2016b, July 11). After the rain. *Walking with Wildlife in Wild Weather Times-A Common World Childhoods Research Collective Blog*. https://walkingwildlifewildweather.com/2016/07/11/after-the-rain/

Taylor, A., & Rooney, T. (2016c, March 20). 'Ngaraka: Shrine for the lost Koori'. *Walking with Wildlife in Wild Weather Times-A Common World Childhoods Research Collective Blog*. https://walkingwildlifewildweather.com/2016/03/20/ngaraka-shrine-for-the-lost-koori/

Vannini, P., Waskul, D., Gottschalk, S., & Ellis-Newstead, T. (2012). Making sense of the weather: Dwelling and weathering on Canada's rain coast. *Space and Culture*, *15*(4), 361–380. https://doi.org/10.1177%2F1206331211412269

Wright, S., Daley, L., & Curtis, F. (2021). Weathering colonisation: Aboriginal resistance and survivance in the siting of the capital. In K. Barry, M. Borovnik, & T. Edensor (Eds.), *Weather: Spaces, mobilities and affects* (pp. 207–221). Routledge.

4
WALKING WITH WEATHER

It's starting to warm up – enough for children to swap their beanies for shade hats – and for underground life to be stirring and emerging on the surface. We spotted our first baby rabbit venturing out of its burrow, and lots of purple spring flowers. Snake season looms and we've told the children it's no longer safe to run into the long tussock grass to play rabbits.

(*Taylor & Rooney, 2016*)

Introduction

In our research, we use specific walking methods, drawing on influences such as Sarah Pink's (2015) sensory ethnographic methods, Tim Ingold's and Jo Lee Vergunst's (2008) walking methods, and Anna Tsing's (2015) more-than-human ethnographic approach of looking to the detail in small and seemingly insignificant human and more-than-human encounters. We walk along with children in ways that attend to the significance of child-weather relations. It turns out that these practices are not only useful as research methods but they also offer pedagogical insight into the potential of this mode of walking for environmental education. The walking techniques we discuss in this chapter can be readily adapted for use in education settings and offer strategies to create learning spaces that foster connection with the complexities and challenges of climate change.

As mentioned in Chapter 1, the two projects drawn on throughout this book ran from 2016 to 2019 and were a research collaboration between the children, families and educators at the University Preschool and Child Care Centre and university researchers. The projects *Walking with Wildlife in Wild Weather Times* (with research team Tonya Rooney and Affrica Taylor) and *Weathering Collaboratory* (with research team Tonya Rooney, Mindy Blaise and Felicity Royds) both had in common a focus on following and noticing children's unfolding relations with

DOI: 10.4324/9781003150411-6

50 Methods: Thinking, moving and writing with weather

more-than-human worlds. The methodology centred around a practice of going on regular walks with a group of approximately 12–15 preschool aged children and their educators, with a new group of children each year. During each year, we would routinely return to places over and over. This was so that the places would become more familiar to the children, allowing them to notice seasonal and other changes over time.

The place where we walked consisted of several acres of urban lakeside environment, featuring grasslands, rocky outcrops, various species of trees, a couple of jetties, a bike path and a view of several buildings (see Figure 4.1).

Part of where we walked has been designated as a conservation area. It includes stretches of grassy woodlands, some of which are remnant areas indicative of pre-settlement vegetation, and which are protected as ecologically endangered communities (Australian National University, 2012, p. 49). Many of the eucalypts and grasses that we encountered have thus weathered colonisation and settlement and provide a glimpse into deep and continuing ecologies of the land.

FIGURE 4.1 Walking place

FIGURE 4.2 Limestone "claw" marks

There are also exposed limestone outcrops, deposited at a time when the region lay under the sea (Australian National University, 2012, p. 42). At these rocks, children would often stop and run their hands over the ridges in the weathered surface (see Figure 4.2).

We wondered if they were sensing something of the forces that shaped these formations. One child suggested they were claw marks of some kind, made by an ancient creature. Features such as these remind us that every landscape has its own histories in geology and biology that in part have been shaped by and with weather, climate and tectonic upheaval.

The site is in many ways an idyllic children's playground – open grasslands to run across, a pebbled beach by the lake to splash about in and stands of trees perfect for climbing. Yet you barely need to scratch the surface to see that it is far from pure or pristine. The water's edge is littered with wind and water swept rubbish (see Figure 4.3), in summer there are "warning – watch out for snakes" signs and we often stumble across dead and rotting animals. The point is not so much that these features make the place any less appealing, but rather that they attest to the fact that all places are at once wild and cultured in an entangled mess that cannot be accounted for by the traditional binary that separates humans from the natural world (Taylor, 2019; Taylor & Pacini-Ketchabaw, 2017). This is similar to how we might understand the air as not always pure and innocent

52 Methods: Thinking, moving and writing with weather

FIGURE 4.3 Wild urban lakeside

but rather the carrier of pollution, smoke or other impurities (Borovnik & Barry, 2021), or vegetation as an entanglement of native and introduced species, noxious weeds or curated gardens. The wildlife includes birds, insects, native grasses and trees, as well as animals and plants with more complex legacies such as rabbits, carp and blackberry bushes (Rooney, 2019a). With Jaime Lorimer (2015), we think of wildlife as not only those creatures who live in wilderness places we imagine as somehow separate from humans but as all the lives and ecologies around us in our messy, urban environment.

Children's encounters with other species throughout our walks were entangled with, rather than separable from, our experience of weather. Children came to know weather through clues such as the activity or stillness of ants, the presence or absence of long grass, mushrooms and fallen leaves. Below, we describe this practice of walking, highlighting both insights into child-weather relations and our reflections on the pedagogical potential of this walking methodology.

Walking as research method

Our more-than-human walking methodology is driven by children's unfolding relations. That is, rather than walking to a destination with predefined expectations of what children might or should learn from the environment, our approach

Walking with weather **53**

is open and drawn by shifting relations between children, worlds and weather. In this chapter, we describe this walking method and some of the challenges and tensions encountered along the way.

When walking with young children outside the confines of the education setting, we notice a sense of joy and curiosity in children's movements as they are drawn along by and with changing weather worlds. In the rain, puddles on the path invite children to splash, jump and sing out loud. An overhanging bush might provide an unexpected hidey-hole that keeps out the glare of the sun or prying adult eyes. The entwined movements of bodies, weather and place suggest something of what Donna Haraway encourages us to attune to through the possibility for joy where "(j)oy is not innocence; it is openness to caring" (cited in Mitman, 2019, p. 19). As children walk, they are drawn along by the world to what is new and unexpected, and in these fleeting moments a new kind of learning becomes possible.

Our walking method is informed by a framework of movement and relationality where worlds are understood as one shared with, and shaped by, relations with human and more-than-human others (Haraway, 2016). During the regular walks, children move along in many ways. They might run, crawl, jump, roll, skip, fall over or lie down. We notice how children are drawn to particular trees, animals, dirt scratchings, flowers, stones, rubbish, bones, insects or animals they encounter when walking along. We do not hurry the group but allow children to linger and be curious about the activities of the microworlds we witness while walking. We also look to the place itself and consider how it draws us in and onwards. We think with Isabelle Stengers (2013) in taking the time to notice what is happening around us and in "learning the art of paying attention" (p. 179). Taking time to notice what is always and already happening is sometimes hard to do in early childhood education because of the developmental logics that privilege the child, her interests and developmental domains of learning. Slowing down with children and being open and attentive to the place around us, is multi-sensory insofar as it involves moving, seeing, touching, listening and smelling. It also extends our ideas of how we understand sensory engagement as "you can listen with your ears, with your nose, with your skin, with your tongue" (Blaise & Hamm, 2022, p. 480). This kind of alertness to the places we walk through is about seeking out and attending to all manner of worldly connections.

Children's movements, invite us to consider Tim Ingold's (2010, p. 130) notion of walking as an "unfolding" where he describes how children move such that their "attention is caught" by the small details they spy along the way. In the discussion below, we extend this notion further by drawing on the work of Lesley Instone (2015) and others to explore the way that place draws children along. We show how walking and being open to the uncertainty of being pulled on by the world, and even being unsure of what a particular walk might *achieve*, is an opportunity for wonder and learning with worlds that would otherwise remain inaccessible to young children.

As mentioned earlier, this mode of walking used in our research also led to unexpected insights for teaching practice. In the next section, we examine more closely the relationship between walking and learning. We follow with a discussion on walking with weather, and the potential of this practice for learning in a climate change era.

Walking as learning

The practice of walking has long been discussed as a reflective opportunity to forge connections with the natural world. More than this, walking also provides a way of coming to know the world in a way that transforms how we think of knowledge itself. In recent years, walking studies (Clement & Waitt, 2017; Ingold & Vergunst, 2008; Springgay & Truman, 2017, 2018) has emerged as a vital, new cross-disciplinary field of research that invites us to think about the physical and sensory engagement between the human body and the places we wander. In contrast to research where walking is a means to move about and observe what is happening, this new form of walking scholarship places an emphasis on the bodily practice of walking as part of what comes to be known and understood (Ingold & Vergunst, 2008; Springgay & Truman, 2017). The suggestion is that, if walking, or moving through a place, is part of how we engage with worlds, then there must be a way in which our moving and sensing bodies contribute to how and what we come to know of worlds (Springgay & Truman, 2017). Embodiment is thus understood as central to knowledge-making, and the movement of bodies is intimately entwined with how we make sense of a particular place, season, experience or time (Springgay & Truman, 2017).

John Horton et al. (2014) suggest that there is much "richness, diversity, intensity and sociability" in the practice of simply "just walking" (p. 111) that matters for children and young people in a way that is often not acknowledged or fully explored in either research or practice. Others have highlighted benefits of going on walks or excursions to open up new modes of learning beyond the classroom. These include the potential for kinaesthetic and sensory learning (Curtis, 2008), embodied learning from place in a way that builds meaning over time (Hackett, 2016), and the potential for speculative world-making made possible at the juncture of movement, art and learning (Springgay & Truman, 2018). These cross-disciplinary contributions suggest there is much to consider in the potential of walking as a pedagogical practice. Recent work by Abi Hackett and Pauliina Rautio (2019) advances this discussion further, arguing that movements such as running or rolling are not just things that children "do" but rather that it is the nonhuman surrounds that invite and prompt certain ways of moving. In a similar vein, we think of walking with young children as a relational practice, where more-than-human worlds are co-constituted by bodies, matter and place.

Thinking of children's movement as entangled with meaning-making offers a starting point for exploring the relationship between walking and learning. There are different modes of walking, and how we think about the practice of

Walking with weather **55**

walking gives rise to different ideas of how children might learn with the world. We start here with Tim Ingold's (2010) notion of "wayfaring". As he explains:

> the wayfarer is a being who, in following a path of life, negotiates or improvises a passage as he goes along. ... his concern is to seek a way through, not to reach a specific destination or terminus but to keep on going. .... Along the way, events take place, observations are made and life unfolds.
>
> (Ingold, 2010, p. 126)

Walking, understood as wayfaring, is much more than simply a way of getting to a destination. It invites a way of coming to know the world in the in-between spaces.

Ingold (2015) differentiates the "wayfarer" from the "navigator" who, in contrast, moves from "point to point" (p. 133). In his description of the navigator, Ingold reminds us of when young children go out on school excursions they are often taught to walk in "crocodile" formation. That is, lined up in pairs, holding hands, not straying to the left or right, and with an adult at the front and rear: "(i)f they pay attention to their surroundings at all, it is in the interests of safety, to avoid collision with traffic or passersby" (Ingold, 2015, p. 130). This mode of walking is about getting to a particular destination and getting there safely; that is, going from point A to point B. The contrast between the wayfarer and the navigator, Ingold suggests, reflects two different views of education. The navigator involves a form of education that draws the learner in; that is, into the rules and representations of culture. The wayfarer, on the other hand, invokes a "drawing out" of the learner into the world where there is "no point of arrival, no final destination, for every place is already on the way to somewhere else" (Ingold, 2015, p. 135). For Ingold therefore, walking understood as wayfaring, invites us to think about "what we learn" as always entwined with the "ways we come to know" and as something that can never be fully grasped or closed as it is always moving on to the next thing (p. 136). The notion of walking as a wayfarer is not just *going to*, but rather a mode of going along and with worlds.

We can take Ingold's idea further by shifting the focus from the learner and how they may be drawn out into the world, to consider how place itself pulls humans to-and-fro and onwards in the world. If we think of place as an entangled and relational exchange with human and more-than-human others, then we can ask different questions about the ways we (humans) come to know and learn with worlds. Rosi Braidotti (2011) observes that "scientific enquiry and exploration has been historically an outward-looking enterprise" (p. 223); an approach that privileges the human sense of entitlement to seek knowledge about and from the world. The challenge, Braidotti suggests, is to find ways to displace this anthropocentric positioning and to build awareness that we (human and nonhuman) are all in this together. In response, we can look to Instone's (2015) contemplation on the relational nature of what it means to walk with (nonhuman) others. Instone (2015) suggests that modes of movement, such as walking, offer an "open and creative mode of being-in-the-world that embraces the

56 Methods: Thinking, moving and writing with weather

twin entanglements of movement and being moved" (p. 135). This is a relational and collective endeavour, where the nonhuman plays a part in drawing out the meaning making that is taking place. Walking in this sense is an opening, a way of finding our way (Instone, 2015); not as humans against the world, nor as a way of coming to know the world only to serve human concerns and desire for knowledge, but as learning with worlds in which we allow ourselves to be drawn by what is challenging or astonishing.

During our fieldwork, we notice that children move along and are moved by various encounters with places, times, weathers and creatures. We recognise this as a form of co-constitution of human and more-than-human bodies, a worlding together which acts as a reminder of Haraway's (2016) notion that "natures, cultures, subjects and objects do not pre-exist their intertwined worldings" (p. 13). The openness in this mode of walking means that children may stumble across things that were never intended or expected. Instone (2015) makes a similar observation as she notes, when walking, there is an "inter-relation between body, knowing, place and feeling that opens the way for surprises and chance encounters" (p. 134). These are the types of encounters that, in a more destination-focused walk, the children might be pulled away from with instructions from adults such as "keep moving" or "don't touch that", leaving behind potentially untapped opportunities for learning with worlds.

Walking along, without concern for a specific destination or purpose, can foster an openness to learning that is driven by both curiosity and a world that draws children on. To follow curiously, is to think of walking as a deeply pedagogical practice where child and worlds let go of knowledge as separable and remain open to the possibilities in collective worlding endeavours. Rebecca Solnit articulates further the significance of a slower kind of walking:

> *Most of the time I go into such landscapes, I walk or run, cutting a line through the landscape, but I learned in the years when I used to gather gallons of blackberries in the tree-shaded gulch through which a creek ran, that there's another kind of depth achieved by moving slow, seeing close-up, lingering, living in detail. You're not trying to get somewhere else but to know where you are.*
>
> *(Solnit, 2021)*

The multi-sensory, imaginative and playful worldly encounters that we noticed on our walks, reveal an intimate entanglement, not just between children and the places we walk but also with weather (see Figure 4.4). On our walks, the lakeside featured as a significant spot for lingering and noticing detail that was often unexpected.

> *The lake edge is mossy and damp, slippery from the recent rain, but children are not deterred. They want to get as close as possible without slipping in. Children reassure each other not to worry about getting a little wet: "The sun can dry you," and "I can*

FIGURE 4.4 Weather surfaces

see the sun reflecting on the water." Bodies lean forward. Lake looms closer. Peering into the watery depths, children see the remains of trees and an array of shiny stones. Looking at the tree debris, they muse: "It's inside the water. Maybe it was too old and then it fell all the way down. It fell into the water and the end is right over there. I see leaves. I can see trees." A hue of sunlight reaches the stones on the lake floor. "What's that under the water? It looks like gold," exclaim the children.

(Adapted from Taylor & Rooney, 2017a)

Sunlight and shadows invited children to test the limits of just how close they could get to the lake without falling in (see similar example in Rooney, 2019b). This captures something of what Ingold (2015) notices as children follow the shifting play of light:

the child's attention is caught — or in the view of the accompanying adult, distracted — by everything from the play of light and shadow to the flight of birds and the barking of dogs, to the scent of flowers, to puddles and fallen leaves.

(p. 130)

However, children are not always drawn to what is quite so idyllic. This mode of walking is not simply "a walk in the park" that reflects childhood innocence in a

58 Methods: Thinking, moving and writing with weather

world of sunlight and shadows (Taylor, 2013). It is messier and more fragmented and more alive with weather affects that are not always pure or contained. Litter caught in the reeds on the edge of the lake catches the children's eye, as they quickly move to imagine new possibilities:

> *Bits of rubbish are floating, drawing children's attention back to the water's surface. A yellow bottle top catches one girls' eye, and she calls out "Golden money!".*
>
> *Soon others gather around: "Where's the golden money? There! We need golden money. But how do we catch it?". With splashing sticks children entreat the bottle-top to come closer. Propelled by current and splashing, the bottle-top floats away. Somewhat ominously a discarded bright yellow container floats nearby with an imprinted black word "DANGER". It is time to leave the rubbish to the whims of wind and water and head back. Shoes and socks are sodden, but no one cares.*
>
> *(Adapted from Taylor & Rooney, 2017b)*

These stories tell of a mode of walking that far exceeds the act of simply moving from one place to the next. In going out and about, along, amongst and with children are responding to worlds they walk through. Affective traces linger within earth, child, soggy socks and the multitude of more-than-human others that the children meet along the way. As the children imagine connections across times and places, they are drawn along by the intimacies of place, materials and a sense of becoming with the world. As educators and researchers, we cannot always be sure what will capture children's attention. It might be a bird or a bug, or something less easy to explain such as dead animals (Taylor, 2019), spider skeletons or dank smells. And while some teachers might be keen to move on from these messy encounters, the children remain fascinated.

In the story above, children are excited and drawn to even the smallest pieces of rubbish floating in the lake. Children understand that the rubbish comes from somewhere else, which on other walks prompts conversations about the entanglement of plastic, birds, fish and turtles. As children move along, learning is illuminated in micro-moments of curiosity; ways of coming to know and be with worlds that might otherwise go unnoticed (Duhn & Galvez, 2020). The relationship between moving and knowing illustrates that learning is taking place through the affective vibrancy and responsiveness of bodies as they are moved by and with place, time, materials and creatures (Bennett, 2010). The stories above show the potential for learning that extends beyond more rigid classroom practices.

A final point to note here is that, when the children journey along the lake, they seem to carry body memories of their previous visit, adding to their anticipation of the delight in reaching the shoreline. Along with others who write of the significance of body memories and their close association with place (for example, Somerville, 2013), we use returning to the same places as one of our strategies for deepening children's understanding of where they are and who and what lives in the place too. By returning to familiar places over time, children come to notice the way things change, as well as what is different or unexpected. When we re-visit some sites, the children are keen to reconnect with what is familiar. But they are also compelled to look closer and start thinking differently about what is happening.

Walking and learning with weather

As we walk along with children, we notice that our movements and encounters are never "weather-neutral" (Vannini et al., 2012) but involve an ongoing negotiation with weather:

> *Having to stray off the path to avoid a puddle or tread more gingerly across a frosty surface to avoid slipping can illustrate how the co-mingling of human-weather relations is evident in even the briefest moments of mobility.*
>
> *(Rooney, 2018, p. 9)*

The ways we move through the world are also how we come to know weather. Ingold (2010) suggests that walking in weather worlds allows us to be open to new ways of knowing through our bodily experience of weather. As we move through weather, we come to know not just the feel of rain or sun on our skin, but the intricacies of the relationship between walking, Earth, bodies and weather. Some have noted the way children respond to changes in the landscape, as in the following example where the researchers observed how "children's movements attune to changes in temperature, light, wind and weather that create micro-variations in the consistency of snow" (Myrstad et al., 2020, p. 9). The weather moves us and the way we move moves weather. Our bodies leave weather traces through shadows cast, scuffed up earth or lines in the snow (Myrstad et al., 2020). Weather also leaves traces on our skin; sunburn, the coolness of a breeze, or an itch from dry summer grass.

Getting to know worldly relations through walking with weather offers a starting point for understanding ourselves as part of, not separate from, weather worlds. Walking in this sense is experimental wandering; a practice we have proposed elsewhere as "a critical and postdevelopmental intervention into a developmentally appropriate or child-centred approach to walking" (Blaise et al., 2019, p. 166). It engages children with learning that is not grounded in facts or from an external positioning to the world, but rather that arises as children move along as part of a mutual shaping of shared worlds. As children imagine and attend to the places they move through, connections are forged and human/nonhuman separations seem to dissolve. We notice a sense of joy, a kind of release of self as becoming with the world. This is similar to what Noora Pyyry (2017) describes in her work on the playfulness of children's experience in urban spaces as "enchantment" or "a feeling of wonder-at-the-world" (p. 1392). We can think of this joy as a mode of learning that

60 Methods: Thinking, moving and writing with weather

Isabelle Stengers (2015) reflects "has something to do with a knowledge, but with a knowledge that is not of a theoretical order" (p. 155).

Conclusion

Some suggest that providing children with open-ended play in an outdoor setting is insufficient on its own to support environmental education (Cutter-Mackenzie et al., 2014). While we agree, we would however add that there are certain ways of being outdoors with children that require both open-ended opportunities and a willingness to work with uncertainty if environmental education is to respond to complex climate worlds and futures. The approach to walking we have described is not a form of intentional teaching with specific learning outcomes but is nonetheless a deliberate and thoughtful practice. It involves giving children an opportunity to walk with, along and amongst outside the confines of an education setting, without a destination in mind, and with time and space to pause, ponder and pursue the worldly encounters that capture their attention, as well as giving space for children to be pursued or drawn on by the world. It is difficult, but important to our approach, to remain with the children and what draws them in and pulls them onwards, and to notice the relations and learnings that might be forged. This shift requires a reorientation of usual teaching practice, which habitually falls into leading by instruction or telling children about what they see. In our walking practice, we still engage children with questions about what they notice, but we work hard to keep questions and possibilities open without overloading this with our own adult frame of reference.

If we are to work with young children in ways that forge deeper connections to and understanding of wider climate worlds, then the potential of walking along with weather offers an opening to learn with and recognise our contribution to the shaping of weather worlds. What is important is not so much the type of place available for walking, but the mode of walking itself; moving as wayfarer or wayfinder who seeks out – or allows oneself to be sought out by – small happenings in the world. We can do this by allowing children time to notice how places and more-that-human others are perhaps seeking us out too and giving children a chance to sense both their own and others' part in a collective worlding endeavour. When we do so, we might also notice the intermingling of movement, earth, children's bodies, ants, rain, mud, rubbish, gumboots and wet socks weathering together within a shared and mutually co-constituted weather world.

Noticing the unfolding weather relations in children's walking encounters, can challenge ideas of what it means to learn. We come to understand that imaginings and moments of joy and astonishment are also forms of knowledge, where the knowing comes from moving with the intricate, and sometimes messy, workings of hidden microworlds. The learning is experimental, curious and suggests a mode of mutual negotiation with weather and worlds.

References

Australian National University. (2012). *ANU heritage study Acton Campus - Volume 1: Heritage study*. Godden Mackay Logan Pty Ltd. https://services.anu.edu.au/files/document-collection/Volume_1_of_the_ANU_Acton_Campus_Heritage_Study.compressed.pdf

Bennett, J. (2010). *Vibrant matter: A political ecology of things*. Duke University Press.

Blaise, M., & Hamm, C. (2022). Lively Emu dialogues: Activating feminist common worlding pedagogies. *Pedagogy, Culture & Society*, 30 (4), 472–489. https://doi.org/10.1080/14681366.2020.1817137

Blaise, M., Rooney, T., & Pollitt, J. (2019). Weather wanderings. *Journal of Public Pedagogies*, (4), 165–170. https://doi.org/10.15209/jpp.1185

Borovnik, M., & Barry, K. (2021). Foggy landscapes. In K. Barry, M. Borovnik, & T. Edensor (Eds.), *Weather: Spaces, mobilities and affects* (pp. 145–158). Routledge.

Braidotti, R. (2011). *Nomadic theory: The portable Rosi Braidotti*. Columbia University Press.

Clement, S., & Waitt, G. (2017). Walking, mothering and care: A sensory ethnography of journeying on-foot with children in Wollongong, Australia. *Gender, Place and Culture: A Journal of Feminist Geography*, 24(8), 1185–1203. https://doi.org/10.1080/0966369X.2017.1372376

Curtis, E. (2008). Walking out of the classroom: Learning on the streets of Aberdeen. In T. Ingold & J. Vergunst (Eds.), *Ways of walking: Ethnography and practice on foot* (pp. 124–143). Ashgate.

Cutter-Mackenzie, A., Edwards, S., Moore, D., & Boyd, W. (2014). A challenge for early childhood environmental education? In A. Cutter-Mackenzie, S. Edwards, D. Moore, & W. Boyd (Eds.), *Young children's play and environmental education in early childhood education* (pp. 1–8). Springer. https://doi.org/10.1007/978-3-319-03740-0_1

Duhn, I., & Galvez, S. (2020). Doing curious research to cultivate tentacular becoming. *Environmental Education Research*, 26(5), 731–741. https://doi.org/10.1080/13504622.2020.1748176

Hackett, A. (2016). Young children as wayfarers: Learning about place by moving through it. *Children & Society*, 30(3), 169–179. https://doi.org/10.1111/chso.12130

Hackett, A., & Rautio, P. (2019). Answering the world: Young children's running and rolling as more-than-human multimodal meaning making. *International Journal of Qualitative Studies in Education*, 32(8), 1019–1031. https://doi.org/10.1080/09518398.2019.1635282

Haraway, D. (2016). *Staying with the trouble: Making kin in the Chthulucene*. Duke University Press.

Horton, J., Christensen, P., Kraftl, P., & Hadfield-Hill, S. (2014). 'Walking… just walking': How children and young people's everyday pedestrian practices matter. *Social & Cultural Geography*, 15(1), 94–115. https://doi.org/10.1080/14649365.2013.864782

Ingold, T. (2010). Footprints through the weather-world: Walking, breathing, knowing. *Journal of the Royal Anthropological Institute*, 16, S121–S139. https://doi.org/10.1111/j.1467-9655.2010.01613.x

Ingold, T. (2015). *The life of lines*. Routledge

Ingold, T., & Vergunst, J. L. (2008). Introduction. In T. Ingold & J. Vergunst (Eds.), *Ways of walking: Ethnography and practice on foot* (pp. 1–21). Ashgate.

Instone, L. (2015). Risking attachment in the Anthropocene. In K. Gibson, D. B. Rose, & R. Fincher (Eds.), *Manifesto for living in the Anthropocene* (pp. 29–36). Punctum Books.

Lorimer, J. (2015). *Wildlife in the Anthropocene: Conservation after nature*. University of Minnesota.

Mitman, G. (2019). *Reflections on the plantationocene: A conversation with Donna Haraway and Anna Tsing* [Audio Podcast]. Edge Effects. https://edgeeffects.net/haraway-tsing-plantationocene/

Myrstad, A., Hackett, A., & Bartnæs, P. (2020). Lines in the snow; Minor paths in the search for early childhood education for planetary wellbeing. *Global Studies of Childhood*, 1–13. https://doi.org/10.1177/2043610620983590

Pink, S. (2015). *Doing sensory ethnography*. (2nd ed). SAGE.

Pyyry, N. (2017). Thinking with broken glass: Making pedagogical spaces of enchantment in the city. *Environmental Education Research*, *23*(10), 1391–1401. https://doi.org/10.1080/13504622.2017.1325448

Rooney, T. (2018). Weather worlding: Learning with the elements in early childhood. *Environmental Education Research*, *24*(1), 1–12. https://doi.org/10.1080/14733285.2018.1474172

Rooney, T. (2019a). Weathering time: Walking with young children in a changing climate. *Children's Geographies*, *17*(2), 177–189. https://doi.org/10.1080/14733285.2018.1474172

Rooney, T. (2019b). Sticking: The lively matter of playing with sticks. In D. Hodgins (Ed.), *Feminist post-qualitative research for 21st century childhoods* (pp. 43–52). Bloomsbury.

Solnit, R. (2021, November 10). In praise of the meander: Rebecca Solnit on letting nonfiction narrative find its own way. *Literary Hub*. https://lithub.com/in-praise-of-the-meander-rebecca-solnit-on-letting-nonfiction-narrative-find-its-own-way/

Somerville, M. (2013). *Water in a dry land: Place-learning through art and story*. Routledge.

Springgay, S., & Truman, S. (2017). A transmaterial approach to walking methodologies: Embodiment, affect, and a sonic art performance. *Body and Society*, *23*(4), 27–58. https://journals.sagepub.com/doi/pdf/10.1177/1357034X17732626

Springgay, S., & Truman, S. (2018). *Walking methodologies in a more-than-human world: Walking lab*. Routledge.

Stengers, I. (2013). Isabelle Stengers in conversation with Heather Davis and Etienne Turpin. In E. Turpin (Ed.), *Architecture in the Anthropocene. Encounters among design, deep time, science and philosophy*, (pp. 171–182). Open Humanities Press.

Stengers, I. (2015). *In catastrophic times: Resisting the coming barbarism*. Open Humanities Press.

Taylor, A. (2013). *Reconfiguring the natures of childhood*. Routledge.

Taylor, A. (2019). Countering the conceits of the Anthropos: Scaling down and researching with minor players. *Discourse: Studies in the Cultural Politics of Education*, *41*(3), 340–358. https://doi.org/10.1080/01596306.2019.1583822

Taylor, A., & Pacini-Ketchabaw, V. (2017). Kids, raccoons, and roos: Awkward encounters and mixed affects. *Children's Geographies*, *15*(2), 131–145. https://doi.org/10.1080/14733285.2016.1199849

Taylor, A., & Rooney, T. (2016). Warming Up. *Walking with Wildlife in Wild Weather Times - A Common World Childhoods Research Collective Blog*. https://walkingwildlifewildweather.com/2016/09/12/warming-up/

Taylor, A., & Rooney, T. (2017a). Lake or sea. *Walking with Wildlife in Wild Weather Times-A Common World Childhoods Research Collective Blog*. https://walkingwildlifewildweather.com/2017/07/19/lake-or-sea/

Taylor, A., & Rooney, T. (2017b). Shifts and flows. *Walking with Wildlife in Wild Weather Times-A Common World Childhoods Research Collective Blog*. https://walkingwildlifewildweather.com/2017/08/16/shifts-and-flows/

Tsing, A. L. (2015). *The mushroom at the end of the world: On the possibility of life in capitalist ruins*. Princeton University Press.

Vannini, P., Waskul, D., Gottschalk, S., & Ellis-Newstead, T. (2012). Making sense of the weather: Dwelling and weathering on Canada's rain coast. *Space and Culture*, *15*(4), 361–380. https://doi.org/10.1177%2F1206331211412269

5
WRITING SMALL WEATHER STORIES

Wind is chilly and leaves us looking for shelter. Overhead birds squawk. Sounds blur with the rush of wind around our ears. A dip in the landscape reveals a spot where creatures might seek relief from harsher elements. With wind, children linger in the small, protected valley. They settle into collecting sticks and leaves to build homes for ants and spiders. Moving and learning with wind is scurrying, bracing and seeking out still places.

(Adapted from Rooney et al., 2019)

Introduction

Talking about *the weather* has long been an entry point into casual conversation; the weather in a particular time and place acts as a point of connection or shared experience of that moment in the world. Add to this the availability of weather apps at our fingertips, and we find ourselves living in a time bursting with ways to talk about the weather. Weather can be deeply personal, with connections to places and memories of events across time and place. Rather than think of stories we might tell about the weather, we can think of *weather as story,* or as one writer expresses this: "weather is a narrative that we wish to tell and retell across time, over and over again" (Adams-Hutcheson, 2021, p. 222).

The sensory and walking methods described in the previous chapter provide an opportunity to notice children's everyday interactions with plants, animals, insects and weather. They also draw attention to weather movements as entwined with knowing and learning. In observing and then writing about children's encounters, we try to challenge the human–centric and outcome–directed positioning that education practice generally tends to bring to how and what we might notice in children's relations with weather worlds. Instead, we remain open and attentive to what emerges in these worldly weather encounters and

DOI: 10.4324/9781003150411-7

64 Methods: Thinking, moving and writing with weather

think carefully about the words, phrases and images we choose when presenting snippets of what we observe. The small weather stories included in this book *(indicated in italics)* come from our field notes, audio recordings, photographic documentation or from the online blogs that form some of the documentation of our projects.

Writing is a creative practice and using an imaginative writing style is a distinct method of feminist scholarship (Braidotti, 2022). Our specific approach to writing small weather stories takes inspiration from Deborah Bird Rose's (2017) poetic prose in the love story she tells between flying foxes and flowers, Donna Haraway's marvellous fabulations with cyborgs (1980, 1991) and her canine companion Cayenne Pepper (2003), Margaret Somerville's (2013) "thinking through Country" methodology that transforms into poetic storytelling and Anna Tsing's (2015) scientific accounts of matsutake mushrooms told through elegant ethnographic narratives. Creating small weather stories is not easy, because it challenges how we have been taught as educators to document children's learning and as researchers to 'write-up' and report ethnographic research. Talking about the weather can help make connections to others, as it grounds us in a familiar or common experience. However, to the extent that such conversations position weather as a separable phenomenon to enjoy, or to contend or deal with, they can limit how we understand our relations with weather and our capacities to live relationally with weather. Writing with weather has meant that we have had to consider how we embed perspectives and voices in our stories, and in particular to think about what may be privileged or silenced in the stories we tell. In doing so, we also provide a point of departure into thinking about the role and practice of documentation in early childhood education, particularly in relation to environmental learning where we bring more-than-human perspectives to expand how we think about child-world relations (Blaise & Rooney, 2020).

All writing is inevitably partial, unfinished and perspective-laden. Through our small weather stories, we aim to show some of the ways children are drawn along by and into worlds as they move. Even though we call these "small stories" it is not so much the length that matters, – they could be two lines or two pages. What is important is that they show the doings and relations of a here-and-now encounter or happening, including connections or relations that surface to and from other times and lives. These small stories also draw from Donna Haraway's storytelling practices and how she:

> *often think[s] in terms of little stories or tiny details or tripping over something that opens up into huge worlds, where thread by thread, as you spin from some tiny thing, you are relooping together the worlds that are required for living and dying here, with these details.*
>
> *(Haraway & Wolfe, 2016, p. 257)*

In other words, the small weather stories we are writing and telling are a practice of connection making.

Our stories follow an emerging practice of telling more-than-human stories in early childhood education and the environmental humanities (Blaise & Hamm, 2022; Blaise & Rooney, 2020; Blaise et al., 2016; Blaise & Wintoneak, 2021; Burarrwana et al., 2019; Haraway, 2016; Pacini-Ketchabaw & Blaise, 2021; Rose et al., 2017; Wintoneak & Blaise, 2022). As Haraway (2016) suggests, possibilities arise when we are open to being led off well-worn paths and to activate stories that might not otherwise be told. Just as the small stories we share here might not have been told otherwise, there will always remain a multitude of other untold stories. It matters though "what stories we tell to tell other stories with" (Haraway, 2016, p. 12), and in early childhood education, the stories we tell in this book reflect the perspectives and possibilities we attend to about weather learning and weathering together.

In taking up the practice of writing small weather stories in an education context, we build on work by others such as Fikile Nxumalo (2016) who tells small stories as a way to decentre the dominant developmental approach in early childhood education which tends to strive for a typical normative or universal *big story* because this is what is considered quality practice. Through small stories, Nxumalo (2016) suggests that there are always things that are uncertain and in-progress that will inevitably and continuously "leak" outside attempts to tell abstract "big" stories. Small stories are more "storied descriptions" (Nxumalo, 2016, p. 40) of partial and unresolvable encounters rather than tales with a neat beginning, middle and end. The small weather stories we tell, are thus an ongoing attempt to practice this type of shift in thinking; that is, one that takes us past abstract progress or "big picture" narratives and instead draws attention to what is curious, unexpected, hidden or even at times seemingly insignificant (Taylor & Pacini-Ketchabaw, 2015; Tsing, 2015).

Like Nxumalo (2016), in our stories we make no attempt to *tidy up* or cleanse our observations for the sake of what might be considered quality practice. Rather, we aim to show some of the small weather happenings and encounters that caught our attention. This is where our storying begins, but more is involved in writing these small weather stories. To say we capture what is partial and complex, is not to say that we don't edit or craft our stories. We do – a lot! At the same time, mindful of Haraway's (2016) call to "stay with the trouble," the work of grappling with and conveying what might seem unclear or incomplete is more than simply a test of writing to distil something coherent from what we notice. It is an ethical call; a call to notice human and more-than-human entanglements and vulnerabilities in the climate disasters that are escalating around the world, and a call to respond and understand how we might share stories that help us to live well together with a multitude of more-than-human others. In this vein, it matters how we privilege and position humans and non-humans in writing about the weather relations we observe. It also matters that we acknowledge these small weather stories are but threads in a wider web of possible stories. These stories often begin with a fleeting moment or happening, which then takes us somewhere else. It is impossible to know where these

66 Methods: Thinking, moving and writing with weather

moments or happenings will go, and we are unable to predict their outcome. It requires us to be open.

Because writing small weather stories is an ongoing creative practice, the weather stories told throughout the book are at different points in their creation; they are all in some way works in progress. Some have been taken directly from research presentations, while others might come from a research blog that we then recrafted by revisiting fieldnotes, photographic documentation and video recordings. Writing small weather stories involves employing a set of creative manoeuvres that have helped us to generate stories showing how children are learning with weather. These manoeuvres influence our entire approach, including how we go about observing children's weather relations, writing them and presenting them to teachers and researchers. While observing, documenting and reporting findings are practices that are expected of both research and teaching, what is different, is the approach we take in relation to perspective, relations, language, listening and the generative potential of storytelling. Our writing is not a linear process. Instead, it involves revisiting stories with ideas and concepts by circling back to new noticings that in turn often lead us elsewhere or that perhaps remain open and incomplete. We regularly review our documentation, paying close attention to how we might have privileged our own perspective and thus challenging us to rethink what we have observed.

This chapter has three sections. First, we explain how we use various creative manoeuvres to compose and craft small weather stories that challenge anthropocentric models of knowledge that separate nature and culture (Oppermann, 2014). Second, we provide an example of how we approach composing and crafting small weather stories as an ongoing, creative and generative practice. Finally, we consider the practice of telling stories *with place* as an extension of our creative writing manoeuvres. We end with an invitation for educators and researchers to take these ideas further in their own documentation practices to see what they offer.

Creative manoeuvres

Creative manoeuvres are not a set of mechanical steps and strategies that we follow to *write-up* small weather stories. Instead, they are part of our writing approach that we have been cultivating over time and in tandem with our walking methodology. Creative manoeuvres are influenced by the decolonising and place-based scholarship carried out in early childhood to represence Indigenous knowledges (see Nxumalo, 2016) and for reimagining human relations with weather.

Creative manoeuvres involve two interrelated strategies of *writing creatively* and *experimentation* that we have found useful for conveying human and more-than-human movements and moments we observe, sense and feel during our research that are simultaneously shaping weather worlds. It is this focus on the simultaneous shaping that is a feminist move because it is contesting the Cartesian dualist model of rationalisms that reinforces mind over matter, object over subject and human over nonhuman, including weather as an object that needs to be separated out as something that is happening *out there*, or to be controlled and managed. Although these creative manoeuvres are interconnected, we present them separately to unpack how we have been composing and crafting small weather stories.

Writing creatively

Our approach to writing is related to our shared interest in creative writing. We have found that paying attention to how we use perspective, language and grammar helps us in telling stories with weather. In particular, this is useful for "animating the animacy" of weather worlds (Chen, 2012). We focus on writing, sometimes with accompanying photos, rather than oral or other visual arts traditions of storytelling, as this reflects our research practice. It is also a practice that holds insights for written documentation in early childhood education as it bears similarities with some of the narrative techniques currently used in pedagogical documentation (Pacini-Ketchabaw et al., 2014).

Perspective

How we approach our observations matters. Shifting from observing and noticing just the child or a single element of weather, towards making room for multiple sense-makings with weather and weather relations is a manoeuvre for letting go of observational traditions and habits that focus the sole emphasis on *the* object or *a* thing. This does not mean ignoring children or things that we see, hear or feel, because acts of meticulous descriptions of puddles, dirt, splashes, sunlight and wind patterns are important for writing specificities. Instead, it is about repositioning how these aspects might inform a story. This manoeuvre recognises the need to approach observations with and from different perspectives or ways of listening, noticing and attuning to make visible multiple weather relations. Considering perspective is fundamental because the very act of observing instantly sets up a divide between us and things, us and relations, and us and worlds. It makes the very idea of us being embedded and part of relations, networks and systems tricky. It is easy to fall into what Donna Haraway (1988) refers to as the god-trick of seeing things from nowhere.

Considering perspective also comes into play when we are crafting small weather stories. For instance, this might entail looking to the significance of weather affects and atmospheres and figuring out how they bring weather learnings together. This is not about writing as if we were a cloud, raindrop or puddle. Instead, it means composing weather stories that account for weather and how this changes all sorts of relations. For instance, rain changes walking tracks from dry and dusty to sludgy, sloppy and sticky; slowing down movements and picking up traces of sticks, pebbles and animals. Some of the

68 Methods: Thinking, moving and writing with weather

ways we do this might involve imagining the liveliness of places, times, plants, rocks, soils and creatures by listening again and again to an audio recording. This often helps us attune to or focus on the sounds of feet stomping in a puddle, while also being reminded how the air was sticky and damp, how it smelled wet in our nostrils and felt sweaty on our fingertips. This attention to multiple sounds activates a flurry of other stories; such as the ways in which one single dew drop captivates a child's attention as it slowly rolls down the eucalyptus leaf, while smothering an ant. Reorienting our focus away from only individual children gives voice to nonhuman vitality. This is not just a literary or stylistic task, but one that involves a mental shift from human-centric positioning and perspective to imagining with the lives and times of more-than-human worlds.

We tell stories of sunlight, warmth, surprise, joy and imagination, and of death, waste, human carelessness, predators and pollution. As we walk along with children, we notice them becoming curious about the lives, vulnerabilities, movements and histories of other worldly inhabitants; often wondering out loud, "look what I've found!", "how did they get here?", "what should I do with this rubbish?", "should I touch that?" or "how did they die?". We still include these voices in our writing, as they are part of how we make sense of such entangled encounters. However, we foreground weather perspectives such as wind and rain, not by imposing human voices or agency on weather, but by acknowledging the mutuality and mingling of weather in the relations we observe.

There is also a collective element to our work, and this is another creative manoeuvre for decentring the all-knowing human expert. Sometimes we (Tonya and Mindy), are able to walk together. And when we are walking, we are also talking and thinking together. Not only are we noticing, listening and attuning, but we are also raising questions and wondering out loud with each other (see also Blaise & Hamm, 2022). This tactic expands our perspective and contributes to attuning to weather relations. Collective reflection also makes it harder to slip back into habits of just noticing and documenting the child. In collective reflection, room is also made to do this with children and with weather. This is similar to the ways in which other research collectives are thinking with place, such as Lesley Instone and Affrica Taylor (2015) collectively thinking with Wee Jasper Valley on Ngunnawal Country, early childhood educators in Canada with Haro Woods et al. (2018) and the Gay'wu group of Indigenous and non-Indigenous women with Rorruwuy, Ḏätiwuy land and Bawaka, Gumatj land (Burarrwanga et al., 2019). We try various manoeuvres to creatively challenge anthropocentric perspectives on knowledge. This is never easy, and it is always imperfect!

Language

Exploring the nature of language and the language of personhood has helped us recognise and accept the limitations of the English language. It has also made clear that language is much more than an empty and neutral vehicle to carry and convey information. Instead of trying to find the right language to pin-down exactly what we hear, see and feel, we are learning how to leave space in our stories to help break the orderly logic of developmentalism that is so readily assumed as the authoritative framework. We have learned to accept that these small weather stories will never be able to represent the full multisensory and textural qualities of the heaviness of rain, or the smell of eucalyptus lingering through the air on a hot summer day.

Through linguistic imperialism, Blaise and Hamm (2019) began recognising how the English language has been imposed over all other languages. Not only has it meant a loss of original Indigenous plant, animal, place and season names (because they might have seemed too hard to pronounce or write), but it is yet another way that humans are distanced from the world. Positioning weather as an object keeps weather and humans separate and renders land as inert (Kimmerer, 2013, 2017). Australia's national broadcaster, the Australian Broadcasting Corporation (ABC) has recently increased its daily use of Indigenous languages and names through several initiatives including the use of Aboriginal and Torres Strait Islander nation names throughout its news reporting, in social media and TV and commissioned screen content as well as incorporating Indigenous place names in several TV and radio programs. One that is of particular interest to us is the inclusion of Indigenous place names in viewer-sourced photographs used in the weather reports of the daily bulletins. This has inspired us to be more deliberate in our future work to use Indigenous place names and seasons when appropriate.

Linguistic imperialism also relegates and assigns pronouns to nonhumans and this reduces plants and animals to an inanimate object. Blaise and Hamm's (2019) writing has been instructive for how they attend to this in their lively story about Stony Creek and White-faced Heron on Wurundjeri Country. Similarly, when writing with weather, we often deliberately refrain from using the specific descriptor "the" (as in "the weather") to avoid any sense of singu-larity or wholeness about weather that might detract from positioning weather as a complex and entangled phenomenon. Taken more broadly, "the" works to position humans and nature as subject-object divides. For example, "I watch 'the' wind move 'the' leaves" distances humans from being embedded with wind as they watch *the* wind move *the* leaves. Although it alerts us to the actions of the wind, it still turns the wind and the leaves into single objects. To counter this, we often do not use "the" in our small weather writing. Instead, we might write "I watch wind move leaves." However, we trouble this phrasing too because it still separates the observer from wind and leaves. After several reworkings, combined with other field notes and photographic documentation we compose the following: "*With wind, children linger in the small, protected valley.*" We are reminded again, of the limitations of the English language and how analysis occurs through the use of creative manoeuvres in our writing. In other words, analysis is so much more than creating common "themes," but instead it is a creative knowledge making process.

70 Methods: Thinking, moving and writing with weather

Grammar

Paying attention to the grammar of animacy has been vital for attending to the significance and liveliness of weather and weather relations and helps us tell lively weather stories. Again, we are guided by how Blaise and Hamm (2019) attend to the grammatical effects of lively nouns, gerunds, pronoun use, and sentence structure to move ideas and activate more-than-human relations in their writing. For us, attending to the grammar of animacy in our small weather stories often, but not always, began by taking a snippet of data from field notes, photographic documentation or an audio clip and then crafting a sentence based on how weather is doing, acting or moving. For instance, *"Wind is chilly and leaves us looking for shelter"* has been written with the grammar of animacy in mind. First, *wind* begins the sentence, making it the subject. Deciding not to write *chilly wind* was deliberate because we wanted the focus to be on wind, from the start of the story. *Chilly* is used to describe the kind of wind, but where it is placed in the sentence matters. Finally, *leaves us looking for shelter*, shows how wind forces bodies to look for shelter.

We also used verbs and gerunds in ways that would animate stories to foreground weather learning and weathering together. This involves paying attention to sentence structure and using verbs and gerunds to privilege active voices or actions, rather than passivity. For instance, *scurrying, bracing and seeking out* gesture towards the active movements created by wind-child relations, and makes room for readers to consider how weather learning occurs.

Experimentation

Experimentation includes an experimental attitude towards a style of writing that is required when confronted with the limits of conventional scholarly prose. Finding ways of writing small weather stories which are full of movements, affects, atmospheres and the unseen, requires us to resist a developmental style of writing that seems to explain too quickly, too easily and too sharply. Although we have been experimenting with writing and storytelling in our own work (Banerjee & Blaise, 2018; Blaise, 2016; Blaise & Wintoneak, 2021; Rooney, 2019; Wintoneak & Blaise, 2022), we recognise that there is a diverse, dynamic, and established field of experimental ethnographic writing (Clifford & Marcuse, 1986; Pandian & McClean, 2017) that has much to teach us.

In this book, each small weather story must find its own form (main character, plot, actions and feelings) to adequately illustrate something of everyday weather-child relations. This often requires an assortment of creative manoeuvres, including trying out new words, playing with perspective and punctuation, listening to how a word or sentence sounds when spoken aloud, re-ordering actions and leaving out some of the details that we originally wrote in our observational field notes. Although we have no recipe for others to follow, we have found that our form of experimentation starts with talking, thinking and writing together.

To do this experimentation, we take insights from various authors who experiment with writing on and with affective, relational and embodied encounters. Lauren Berlant and Kathleen Stewart (2019), for example, have taught us ways to describe what *might be* happening on our walks, how to notice weather unfoldings and how to hold weather moments together. Holding onto weather moments is hard to do because they are often fleeting and unclear. In addition, the field of early childhood education expects teachers and researchers to know exactly what is going on in the learning environment, or what a child is learning, and what they need to do next. All of these ways of knowing expect us to pin-down what we observe, hear and feel; and to be certain. Holding onto feelings, sensations and inklings, requires the ability to not know and to speculate "what if."

The use of poetics and broad poetic explorations in experimental ethnographic and environmental writing to compose lively, enmeshed and hybrid worlds has been instructive in helping us to do lively weather writing. We are just beginning to experiment with poetics and are developing a poetic mindedness (Pendergast, 2009). This is useful and Debora Bird Rose's poetic approach across her work teaches us the importance of rhythm, rhyme, form and metaphor in our writing as we continue to experiment and compose small weather stories that attend to weather temporalities, pressures, movements and affects. In doing so, our writing becomes more performative and intends to do *something* to readers.

Finally, speculation is another strategy that we use in our writing. Similar to the ways in which children practiced imagining while they were walking, noticing and becoming with weather worlds, we too speculate to compose small weather stories. Children's abilities to wonder about what might be or could be happening in weather worlds is a creative manoeuvre that opens-up space for understandings, rather than closing them down. These diverse styles of expression bring our writing into a collaborative and iterative space – a space of making worlds by giving voice to possibilities and other perspectives. Writing is part of the *doing* in world making.

Writing small weather stories

The creative manoeuvres described above help bring weather and weather relations to the foreground. To show how this might be done, we share another short story, and explain how it was developed over several drafts. On wet rainy days, when the children rush ahead to seek out puddles and then splash with pure joy, there seems to be so much to say about weather–child relations, yet it can be hard to write all the happenings of these small moments (see Figure 5.1).

Never really knowing exactly where to start, we might begin composing with the following short sentences:

> *Amy jumps in puddles, making a mess everywhere. She has fun even though her shoes get muddy.*

FIGURE 5.1 Muddy puddles

In this description, the child is the central agent. She is doing and causing everything. Things also happen to her, and she is the only being or thing that is named. To further develop this as a short weather story, we can re-draft as follows:

> *Children jump in puddles. Water splashes into the air and mud sticks to children's clothes. The air fills with joyful sounds.*

In this version, child, weather and water are all afforded the same agency. The child is not named which helps to indicate that it is not the child's individual development we are focusing on. Other things and existents are also expressed without using "the" as an object identifier. We learn of the actions and effects of water as something distinct from the child's actions. There is more of a level playing field in the way the encounter is observed and documented. After reading these sentences out loud, we trouble and discuss our use of "the" in the second and third sentences. In the end we decide that for this small weather story, including "the" in both sentences works towards keeping the focus on the relational happenings between air, water and sounds.

As part of our process, we would next ask, how can we improve this further to achieve an even stronger sense of relationality and mutuality? Here is the next draft:

Rain has settled in patches and draws children away from the dry path. Splash, splash! Water whooshes higher and higher and mud splatters over boots and raincoats. A new song becomes a refrain for the rest of our walk, "muddy puddles, muddy puddles."

In this draft, we give voice to the way that place and weather draw children onwards. The puddles act as an invitation to weather together with rain, Earth and the making of mud. By mentioning the song the children sing, we not only convey their joy, we also get a sense that this is a weather encounter that they carry with them long after the splashing and jumping. One more thing we can add to our story is a sense of open-endedness or unanswered questions.

Rain has settled and draws children away from the dry path. Splash, splash! Water whooshes higher and higher and mud splatters over boots and raincoats. We notice Earth being shaped by stomping and stamping. Human presence marks the land. As children jump higher, they seem to test the limits of their discomfort. We wonder if they recognise their vulnerability to the whims of weather as they resist getting too wet on this cold day.

Here, we draw attention to the mutually generative aspects of the relations between child, land and weather. We also speculate and raise questions that we cannot know the answer to, as we do not have insight into this from either child or muddy puddles. Our wonderings mingle with the short weather stories we share and can help, over time, to build new ways of noticing and knowing the weather worlds we walk through. The practice of writing and re-writing is part of this process.

This example is one of the ways in which we can revise, rewrite, notice different textures and senses and retell small weather stories. This is not so much a linear process for developing this style of writing, but rather one where we try to bring in distinct shifts in perspective, grammar and language and where we experiment with these and other elements. This approach can be adopted in relation to a single piece of writing, or it can extend over the course of several projects.

Drawing on the writing practices described above, there is much that can be used to develop more experimental techniques for documentation in early childhood education. A willingness to employ and test out creative manoeuvres might help to capture some of the deeper moments of learning in children's emerging relations with worlds and weather.

Storying with place and weather

Not all stories are human stories to tell, and not all human stories are ours to tell. As already mentioned, we cannot do justice to the multitude of tales that might be told. We can however benefit from reflecting on the way that stories come

74 Methods: Thinking, moving and writing with weather

into the world and form part of children's learning. We can also think about how stories are told not just through words, song and art, but through place, rivers, mountains, weather and other beings and matter. From our earlier discussion on *Song Spirals*, it is possible to think of how stories might not just be told by people, but also by and through the places we live. The Gay'wu group of women speak from their place. We hear that place matters:

> *This tells us that we can only speak from our place. It tells us that place is always important. When we do milkarri or sing the songspirals, we are singing from our own place.*
>
> *(Burarrwanga et al., 2019, p. 109)*

The women also convey a sense of how stories are told across life and death, and over times:

> *So the songspirals, which bring Country into existence, are deeply connected to people. It is a profoundly deep connection, much more than a lifestyle.*
>
> *(Burarrwanga et al., 2019, p. 39)*

The relationship between story, place, time, knowledge, people and song is important, and invites us to consider in what ways stories might be told with and by place and weather.

Through reading *Song Spirals*, we have learned new words of singing and storying, and have come to understand there are deeper ways of knowing language and land. While we can listen only on the surface, many of the ideas resonate and we become curious. The singing is telling stories of, with and through Country:

> *When we keen or cry, it's a story we are telling. It's telling a story in keening. …It brings us back to the moment. It is the present, the past and the future. If we are singing about the rain coming down to the land, we become part of that water that drops to the soil, that sinks into the soil.*
>
> *(Burarrwanga et al., 2019, p. 257)*

We notice that the book *Song Spirals* is written in a non-linear way. Stories spiral, with each story adding a new dimension or perspective that builds up slowly as the reader listens. Parts of stories are retold, but with new or slightly different detail. There is a type of layering at work in this story writing; a way of telling stories with Country that also make Country, and of passing on stories that are also part of the stories that are passed on. Telling stories through these layers is not something we can replicate. But as the book continues spiralling and adding meaning as the story moves along, we are reminded of the movement of water and wind, carrying the story (meanings and knowledges) onwards and back again and around. Spirals wind gradually and continuously, picking up ideas along the way, while dropping others. We reflect on what it might mean to tell stories with place, water and wind. How might we tell stories that encourage layers and multiple voices, rather than linear narratives that move from beginning to end with little room to revisit or circle back to things as they matter or surface?

Another feature we notice about the telling of stories in *Song Spirals,* is that direction or perspective is important.

> *As we walk, we turn our head from side to side, looking for and thinking of our place. We are attending to what is there, to the beings and belongings of Country, to our kin, to our land.*
>
> *(Burarrwanga et al., 2019, p. 80)*

Of course, there must be something significant about the way we turn our heads or where we face as we walk along; something that matters for how and what we attend to and think with. Yet, it was not until we read these words from *Song Spirals,* that we realised how this mattered in the telling of stories. Turning, thinking and looking is part of how we notice and relate to the places we walk and therefore critical to the stories we might tell. The women explain further: "This is the songspiral. It is walking, head turning, looking, noticing, thinking as we watch the land, paying attention, with love. Walking in kinship" (Burarrwanga et al., 2019, p. 81).

Reading these stories prompted us to consider more fully what it is that Isabelle Stengers (2015) means when she encourages us to *make ourselves pay attention.* Stengers wants us to look beyond what appears immediately note-worthy and to notice what might be neglected or over-looked. Further, she is not suggesting we look out for things that are *a priori* defined as important, but rather to turn our attention to "something that creates an obligation to imagine, to check, to envisage, consequences that bring into play connections between what we are in the habit of keeping separate" (Stengers, 2015, p. 62). In the context of climate change, these ideas are important in helping us to attend to connectedness rather than separability, and to consider the ethical dimensions in the choices we make when paying attention.

Conclusion

We can no longer ignore what is difficult or no longer smooth over the stories we tell of and from children's encounters with weather and worlds. The colonisation of weather and the political discourses surrounding climate change, highlight how stories of weather will always be also ethical and political. This does not mean that we need to engage in confronting and fear-inducing tales, but rather that we need to make the time and place for grappling with questions that may not have easy answers. Indeed, the practice of giving room to such opportunities, and being unsure what will emerge – such as on our outdoor walks with young children, is in itself an act of resistance against

76 Methods: Thinking, moving and writing with weather

the tendency to abstract or conjure up whole truths in a neat and tidy education package. As Affrica Taylor (2017) argues, such an approach to education allows us to respond to the "real, messy and non-innocent cosmopolitical worlds in which we actually live" (p. 61). Thinking with where and how stories are told, and who tells stories, also helps us to understand stories as part of what is happening. Fikile Nxumalo (2018) describes "worlding as a mode of storying" where worldings are emergent and allow us to look out for what "eludes easy representation" (p. 150). One of the ways in which the dominant discourse of developmentalism is being challenged is through decolonising the colonial places and spaces in early childhood education. Veronica Pacini-Ketchabaw and Affrica Taylor (2015) show how early childhood education is a part of, not somehow separated off from, the social and ecological legacies of colonialism and Nxumalo (2019) has been developing storying practices to refigure quality in early childhood education. We are inspired by the ways in which Nxumalo brings together various theoretical figurations of witnessing to engage and dialogue with place politically. Her storied practices of witnessing place specificities and cross-species socialities show us ways we might go about disrupting ongoing colonialism through further development of our writing practices.

Stories thus move and are moved, and in telling our child-weather stories in writing we try to capture something small as a performative and collaborative gesture to weather worlds. We have slowly come to understand stories as a type of *doing* or *making* in themselves, and yet we still limit our modes of expression to words and photos. Sometimes the language is hard to craft; perhaps this is because we think too much of language as words on the page rather than voices, callings, doings and happenings.

Children tell stories too. On our walks they often sing as they wander along. Where do their songs come from; the movement between body and land; a relaxing of rigid boundaries; a desire to sing with land and rain? We don't know the answers, but we do notice the singing. When children linger in a particular place, if we listen closely, we can also hear them talking to animals, seeds and rain: "Here let me make a home for you," "I'll help you grow" or just a simple "Hello." Sometimes this conversation feels two-way (except that we cannot hear the response). As children converse with nonhuman companions, we sense a collaborative storying between child and place. Stories without a beginning or end, but somehow snippets woven into shared worlds. Thinking, walking and writing with weather and children has brought us closer to the intimacies and activities of weather worlds. Perhaps with this proximity, we might find clues as to what it means to live well with weather and climate – and in turn, what learning and teaching might entail in this context.

In the next part of the book, we examine more closely human relations with weather that we have noticed on our walks with children. In doing this, we hope to provide ways and words for us to recognise and forge ongoing weather entanglements – through bodies, materials, times and places.

References

Adams-Hutcheson, G. (2021). Dwelling and weather: Farming in a mobilised climate. In K. Barry, M. Borovnik, & T. Edensor (Eds.), *Weather: Spaces, mobilities and affects* (pp. 222–235). Routledge.

Banerjee, B., & Blaise, M. (2018). An unapologetic feminist response. *Research in Education, 101*(1), 17–24. https://doi.org/10.1177/0034523718792163

Berlant, L., & Stewart, K. (2019) *The hundreds.* Duke University Press.

Blaise, M. (2016). Fabricated childhoods: Uncanny encounters with the more-than-human. *Discourse: Studies in the Cultural Politics of Education, 37*(5), 617–626. https://doi.org/10.1080/01596306.2015.1075697

Blaise, M., & Hamm, C. (2019). Shimmering: Animating multispecies relations with Wurundjeri Country. In, D. Hodgins (Ed.), *Feminist post-qualitative research for 21ˢᵗ century childhoods* (pp. 93–100). Bloomsbury.

Blaise, M., & Hamm, C. (2022): Lively Emu dialogues: Activating feminist common worlding pedagogies. *Pedagogy, Culture & Society, 30*(4), 472–489. https://doi.org/10.1080/14681366.2020.1817137

Blaise, M., Hamm, C., & Iorio, J. M. (2016). Modest witness(ing) and lively stories: Paying attention to matters of concern in early childhood. *Pedagogy, Culture and Society, 25*(1), 31–42. https://doi.org/10.1080/14681366.2016.1208265

Blaise, M., & Rooney, T. (2020). Listening to and telling a rush of Unruly Natureculture gender stories. In F. Nxumalo & C. P. Brown (Eds.), *Disrupting and countering deficits in early childhood education* (pp. 151–163). Routledge. http://dx.doi.org/10.4324/9781315102696-10

Blaise, M., & Wintoneak, V. (2021). (Re)forming river–child–blowie relations: Questions of noticing, caring and imagined futures with the unloved and disregarded. *Feral Feminisms: Hacking the Anthropocene Do-It-Together (DIT), 10*(Fall), 137–145.

Braidotti, R. (2022). *Posthuman feminism.* Polity Press.

Burarrwanga, L., Ganambarr, R., Ganambarr-Stubbs, M., Ganambarr, B., Maymuru, D., Wright, S. L., Suchet-Pearson, S., & Lloyd, K. (2019). *Songspirals: Sharing women's wisdom of Country through songlines.* Allen & Unwin.

Chen, M. Y. (2012). *Animacies: Biopolitics, racial mattering, and queer affect.* Duke University Press.

Clifford, J., & Marcuse, G. E. (Eds) (1986). *Writing culture: The poetics and politics of ethnography.* University of California Press.

Haraway, D. (1988). Situated knowledges: The science question in feminism and the privilege of partial perspective, *Feminist Studies, 14*(3), 575–599. http://www.jstor.org/stable/3178066

Haraway, D. (2003). *The companion species manifesto: Dogs, people and significant otherness.* Prickly Paradigm Press.

Haraway, D. (2016). *Staying with the trouble: Making kin in the Chthulucene.* Duke University Press.

Haraway, D. J., & Wolfe, C. (2016). Companions in conversation. In D. Haraway (Ed.), *Manifestly Haraway* (pp. 199–296). University of Minnesota Press.

Haro Woods, Nelson, N., Yazbeck, S. L., Danis, I., Elliott, D., Wilson, J., Payjack, J., & Pickup, A. (2018). With(in) the forest: (Re)conceptualizing pedagogies of care. *Journal of Childhood Studies, 43*(1), 44–59. https://doi.org/10.18357/jcs.v43i1.18264

Instone, L., & Taylor, A. (2015) Thinking about inheritance through the figure of the Anthropocene, from the Antipodes and in the presence of others. *Environmental Humanities, 7*(1), 133–150. https://doi.org/10.1215/22011919-3616371

Kimmerer, R. W. (2013). *Braiding sweetgrass: Indigenous wisdom, scientific knowledge, and the teaching of plants.* Milkwood Edition.

78 Methods: Thinking, moving and writing with weather

Kimmerer, R. W. (2017, June 12). Speaking of nature: Finding language that affirms our kinship with the natural world, *Orion Magazine*, https://orionmagazine.org/article/speaking-of-nature/

Nxumalo, F. (2016). Storying practices of witnessing: Refiguring quality in everyday pedagogical encounters. *Contemporary Issues in Early Childhood*, 17(1), 39–53. https://doi.org/10.1177/1463949115627898

Nxumalo, F. (2018). Stories for living on a damaged planet: Environmental education in a preschool classroom. *Journal of Early Childhood Research*, 16(2), 148–159. https://doi.org/10.1177/1476718X17715499

Nxumalo, F. (2019). *Decolonising place in early childhood education*. Routledge.

Oppermann, S. (2014). From ecological postmodernism to material ecocriticism: Creative materiality and narrative agency. In S. Iovino & S. Oppermann (Eds), *From ecological postmodernins to material ecocriticism: Creative materiality and narrative agency* (pp. 21–36). Indiana University Press.

Pacini-Ketchabaw, V., & Blaise, M. (2021). Feminist ethicality in child-animal research: Worlding through complex stories. *Children's Geographies*. https://doi.org/10.1080/14733285.2021.1907311

Pacini-Ketchabaw, V., & Taylor, A. (eds.) (2015). *Unsettling the colonial places and spaces of early childhood education*. Routledge.

Pacini-Ketchabaw, V., Nxumalo, F., Kocher, L., Elliot, E., & Sanchez, A. (2014). *Journeys: Reconceptualizing early childhood practices through pedagogical narrations*. University of Toronto Press.

Pandian, A., & McClean, S. J. (Eds) (2017). *Crumpled paper boat*. Duke University Press.

Pendergast, M. (2009). "Poetry is what?": Poetic inquiry in qualitative social science research. *International Review of Qualitative Research*, 1(4), 541–568.

Rooney, T. (2019) Weathering time: Walking with young children in a changing climate. *Children's Geographies*, 17(2), 177–189, DOI: 10.1080/14733285.2018.1474172

Rooney, T., Blaise, M., & Royds, F. (2019). Manifesto: Weathering-with wind, Shaping new pedagogies in times of climate change. Presented at the *American Educational Research Association Conference*, Toronto, Canada, April, 2019.

Rose, D. B. (2017). Shimmer: When all you love is being trashed. In A. L. Tsing, H. A. Swanson, E Gan, & N. Bubandt (Eds), *Arts of living on a damaged planet: Ghosts and monsters of the Anthropocene* (pp. G51–G63). University of Minnesota Press.

Rose, D. B., van Dooren, T., & Chrulew, M. (2017). *Extinction studies: Stories of time, death and generations*. Columbia University Press.

Somerville, M. (2013). *Water in a dry land: Place-learning through art and story*. Routledge.

Stengers, I. (2015). *In catastrophic times: Resisting the coming barbarism*. Open Humanities Press.

Taylor, A. (2017). Beyond stewardship: Common world pedagogies for the Anthropocene. *Environmental Education Research*, 23(10), 1448–1461. https://doi.org/10.1080/13504622.2017.1325452

Taylor, A., & Pacini-Ketchabaw, V. (2015). Learning with children, ants, and worms in the Anthropocene: Towards a common world pedagogy of multispecies vulnerability. *Pedagogy, Culture & Society*, 23(4), 507–529. https://doi.org/10.1080/14681366.2015.1039050

Tsing, A. L. (2015). *The mushroom at the end of the world: On the possibility of life in capitalist ruins*. Princeton University Press.

Wintoneak, V., & Blaise, M. (2022). Voicing Derbarl Yerrigan as a feminist anti-colonial methodology. *River Research and Applications*, 3(3), 435–442. https://doi.org/10.1002/rra.3822

PART III

Relations: Weathering with more-than-human worlds

6

BODIES, ATMOSPHERES AND AFFECTS

Wind is invisible. Its presence is known through shifts in the landscape, such as swirling dust or choppy water on the lake or in the forms of eucalypts sculpted gradually over time. Children become wind when they throw autumn leaves up and watch them fall. Wind makes children pull their coats and beanies tighter. Wind and children shift and shape each other as they move along.

(Rooney et al., 2019)

Introduction

Lake and child have a compelling relationship that we have observed as children return time and again, often reluctant to leave. There is an ongoing entanglement of weather bodies in children's encounters with swan bodies, stone bodies, grass bodies, litter bodies as well as rippling reflections of sun and wind across the body of water. Drawing from feminist ideas of embodiment (Grosz, 1994) and trans-corporeality (Alaimo, 2010) we consider how atmospheres and elements are moving through and with bodies as weather bodies (Pollitt et al., 2021). Rain, heat, wind, shadows and clouds are not just outside the preschool waiting for children to observe or measure. They are inside too, blurring how we think about the material divide between inside and outside. For one thing, weather transverses this boundary when sunlight and warmth filter across the floor or wind whistles under the door. Child, weather and more-than-human weather bodies are mingling and moving across each other. Affects of weather linger on bodies and clothes as children move around. Weather is not readily *locked out* by a wall; a structure itself constructed from weathered timbers that continue to weather the elements. Weather is also not readily contained outside a body. As we have reported elsewhere (Pollitt et al., 2021), when children are asked what weather they can sense in their bodies, they respond variously

DOI: 10.4324/9781003150411-9

FIGURE 6.1 "There's a sun in my tummy"

with descriptors such as "'Stormy!' 'Blue skies with birds tweeting' 'Snowing!' 'Sunny'" (p. 1146) (see Figure 6.1).

These are all small examples in some respects, but by considering more deeply the mingling, exposing and composing of bodies, materials and atmospheres (Alaimo, 2016), we can identify new possibilities in the way children might forge connections to wider shifts in climate. Touch, smell, taste, sound and a rich kaleidoscope of colours and textures, invite attention to weather worlds, often as if seeing or feeling (and hence coming to know) them anew.

In this chapter, we begin with a brief survey of some of the research that has informed our thinking on the sensory and bodily dimensions of weather learning. We then share findings from our work with children where we have practiced "atmospheric attunement to the elemental" (Gannon, 2016) as a way of understanding how humans not only feel weather, but *are* weather, such as via the porosity of skin and bodies. Through two stories, *Rain songs* and *Dead fish*, we highlight the curious and disconcerting affects in the sensory relationship between human bodies, water bodies, fish bodies and weather bodies. We tell of interactions that might variously be experienced as comfort or discomfort, anticipated or unexpected, familiar or new. At the same time, we try to (re)imagine these experiences from a more-than-human perspective, calling into question the notion that weather *does things to us* in ways that are unidirectional, linear and

Bodies, atmospheres and affects **83**

immediately knowable. Instead, we suggest, there are trans-corporeal, sensorial and affective dimensions to how children learn with weather; ways of knowing that are entangled with other weather bodies and where questions remain unanswered even as weather learning accumulates in and through children's bodies. We end the chapter with a discussion that draws together bodies, atmospheres and affects, and consider implications for education pedagogy and practice.

Weather affects

The affective engagement between body and weather is familiar, yet complex, and is more than the sensations or emotions bound up in a particular weather encounter. As Philip Vannini and colleagues (2012) remind us:

> *We sense weather in the present moment, but our sensations are shaped by sensory skills that are informed by both past memories and future expectations. In sum, perceptions of the weather are difficult to articulate, and its sensory experience is just as complex.*
>
> *(p. 368)*

Moving along with and through weather worlds is a sensory experience, and one that helps us to make sense of the world (Vannini et al., 2012). Other research draws attention to the way that sensory weather experiences can stay with children. Zsuzsa Millei and colleagues (2019) describe how children's bodies can become attuned to certain types of climatic environments when they return to these over again. Icy environments, for example, energise and transform bodies "including human bodies and nonhuman objects, animals, sun and wind, warm and cold, sand and snow, skis and skates, and helmets and woollen socks" (Millei et al., 2019, p. 60). It is through weather that such environments "linger in children's bodies in the form of presence" (Millei et al., 2019, p. 60). The affective traces of weather do not just pass over the surface of skin. Rather, weather permeates and affective responses arise from within bodies. These can range from a sense of discomfort to pure joy. Susannah Clement (2021), in her study on parents taking young children out and about, explains how for one mother, rain can disrupt the "affective resonance of bodily comfort needed to make a walk to the park enjoyable for her and her children" (p. 57), while at other times, rain – and the opportunity for children to jump in puddles – can turn an uncomfortable walk into a "joyful transgression" (Clement, 2021, p. 59). In these types of sensory encounters, we can see much deeper affects at work than a transitory meeting with weather. Via our skin, elements such as rain, wind and sunshine leave traces in bodies (Clement & Waitt, 2017). We carry weather affects along to other places and times (Rooney, 2019a), traces accumulate (Millei et al., 2019) and attuning to weather can come to be understood as a practice of tracing ecologies and histories that surface and challenge us to think differently (Banerjee & Blaise, 2013; Flikke, 2019; Hohti et al., 2021).

84 Relations: Weathering with more-than-human worlds

It is not always easy to make sense of the weather, particularly in the context of sometimes erratic and extreme weather events. Susanne Gannon (2016) experiments with thinking about how the small, almost indiscernible, shifts in weather and atmosphere can shape both spaces and the relations within those spaces. Gannon (2016) explains that everyday weather events – such as the fall of light across the ground or gutters filling with water – might seem trivial. Yet, if we can find ways of attending more closely to these, then this might offer a mode of connection to larger climate change events that also demand our attention. Citing Jackson and Fannin (2011), Gannon (2016) explains that, in the context of climate change, "we have 'no choice but to listen,' but we need to listen differently, and with all our senses, to better understand how we are immersed within the 'fragile balances of earth, air, water, and fire'" (p. 86).

In thinking about how we might listen differently, we can also note the work of Bettina Hauge (2013), who in writing on the phenomenon of air, explains that air "is a way of studying our relationship with the environment" (p. 172). Based on a study of the daily practices of bringing fresh air into homes, Hauge notes that our relationship with air is not only a sensory and bodily experience but is deeply entwined with care and well-being via small daily tasks such as opening windows for ventilation or hanging washing out to dry. Pollution and other impurities cause us to question the freshness of the air we breathe, drawing attention to the "messier" and "mixed-up" aspects of air (Tammi, 2019). And the irony of a blast of "free" cool air from an airconditioned mall raises confronting questions about the relationship between human comfort, air temperature and greenhouse gas emissions (Banerjee & Blaise, 2013). We might also consider the way that buildings *breathe* through ventilation systems (Tammi, 2019) or how certain clothes are designed to breathe; in both regards, the materials are used to moderate air, humidity and temperature to maximise comfort for humans in inclement conditions. Everyday atmospheres are thus present across our lives, including choices about the clothes we wear or the buildings in which we take shelter – so much so that we often take them for granted. Through small daily interactions with air, Hauge (2013) notes that "air has a dynamic force of its own and makes people part of, connect to and reflect upon the environment" (p. 182). These ordinary sensory modes of connection to weather might therefore offer important ways to understand the shifts and changes in the wider climate worlds we inhabit.

Attuning to the weather as a sensory and bodily practice has a political dimension too. While the affects of weather might offer a personal connection to what is an ordinary or everyday experience, if we understand this phenomenon through Kathleen Stewart's (2007) work on "ordinary affects" we can come to understand these experiences as a kind of "contact zone" to social spaces, events and technologies where "flows of power literally take place" (p. 2). That is, the affects of weather are more than an individual bodily experience or sensation. We only need to look at the comforts and discomforts of weather associated with housing accessibility, work conditions or indoor air control systems to

Bodies, atmospheres and affects **85**

see patterns of power and privilege at work (Tammi, 2019). We can also look to Mel Y Chen's (2012) scholarship on affect and the flows of power that this entails, as they explain:

> *I include the notion that affect is something not necessarily corporeal and that it potentially engages many bodies at once, rather than (only) being contained as an emotion within a single body. Affect inheres in the capacity to affect and be affected.*
> *(Chen, 2012, p. 11)*

We get a sense here that there is something that matters in "how one body affects another" (Chen, 2012, p. 12). This is reinforced in Rune Flikke's (2019) historical and contemporary accounts of air and atmospheres in colonial societies in southern Africa which shows how air can link the social, temporal and conceptual scales to illuminate contemporary material politics of air. By showing how affect engages many bodies at once, Chen's interdisciplinary scholarship helps us to understand the multiplicities of atmospheric affects. This helps us to recognise the affects of weather as more than an individual or unidirectional sensation, but rather as affective flows between entities that cannot be disentangled from power, politics and sociality.

Collecting or capturing the affects of weather is a patchy and imperfect process. Bringing attention to the ordinary, without trying to arrive at a full theory as to what these insights might offer, is one of the many ways in which we employ feminist methods in our weather work. We take inspiration from Stewart's (2007) work here, to try to seek out the "intensities of the ordinary through a close ethnographic attention" as a way of trying to find points of "curiosity, impact and encounter" (p. 5). We may (or may not) unearth the flows of power or politics that thread through these moments, but at the very least we hope to show how attending to the affects of weather can reveal just how connected we are all to air, water, atmospheres and the human presences that swirl through weathers and climates. In these small moments, we might witness some of the shifts, histories and powers bound up in the shaping of wider weather worlds.

Traces of two weather encounters

The following stories highlight the mingling of children's bodies, atmospheres and weathering, drawing attention to the sensory and affective relations that children experience with and through weather. We follow these with a discussion on how and why such encounters can be seen as a form of weather learning that promotes connection with complex and often puzzling, weather worlds.

Rain songs

> *Children test out the feel of raindrops and draw in smells from the damp earth. Those with gumboots rush to jump in puddles. Those without are a bit more cautious, but*

*inevitably end up with wet shoes and socks. We notice chatter and singing when the
rain begins. A mix of familiar and invented tunes fill the air.*

> "Raaain! It's too rainy, we have to go inside."
> "I'm going to get a cold because we haven't got any jackets."
> "I like rain because it makes puddles."
> "I felt a raindrop land on my leg."
> "I felt a raindrop on my hair!"
> "Me too."
> Children sing along, by themselves, with each other, with birds and with rain. "Rain
> rain, go away, come again another day... rain rain go away, don't come back another
> day... yea yea yea-yea yea, we don't want you."
> "Magpie... Stick with the group."
> "Did we scare the magpie?"
> "I feel lots of raindrops."
> "I just felt four!"
> (Children singing) "So many raindrops. So many raindrops."
> (More children singing) "Rain, rain, go away, come again another day."
> "It still isn't working. That song sometimes works."
> "Even my shirt is getting wet!"
> "I can see rain here. In the ground."
> "I can see rain up there." (Child pointing at clouds)
>
> (F. Royds, field note, 2 November 2018)

In the midst of the enthusiasm, children shifted between wanting to stay in
the rain and thinking about heading back to the preschool. Singing familiar
refrains such as "rain, rain, go away," never really seemed to be about going
back, but more a way of going on with rain. As noted in the previous chapter,
on our walks it wasn't unusual for one or more of the children to break out
into a spontaneous made-up song that accompanied the rhythm of our walk.
Such expressions seemed to come out of the blue, and yet when we looked at
how the children were moving and being moved, it was perhaps not surprising. Rain was an invitation to attend more closely to what might otherwise
be missed, or soon be gone (Rooney, 2019b). Children *talked* or sang *to* rain
and tried to tell rain what to do. They reflected on whether rain was listening
or not – "that song sometimes works" – they observed. We wondered if and
how rain might listen or reciprocate to this rush of sensory and conversa-
tional interchange? In the mingling of sound, movement, smells, air and water,
we also thought of the ways that air and rain were part of the songs being
sung. As the movement of walking in and with rain flowed through children's
conversations, we were reminded of the creative work *Conversations with Rain*
(Pollitt et al., 2019) where children were invited to participate in "opportunities for sensing, noticing, breathing, wondering and experimenting toward
open-ended imaginative outcomes" (n.p.) with rain as an alternative to more
didactic approaches to learning about climate change. We too are interested
in the learning potential of the children's sing-song encounters as they walk
with rain. Perhaps these small encounters might open-up connections that

transverse bodily boundaries and linger on skin and clothes; connections to other climate and weather worlds.

On our walks, rain acted as an invitation for children to splash in puddles or kneel to investigate the sponginess of grass. Screwing up her nose, one child declared that the rain made everything smell "*disgusting*," like "*yucky wet poo*." Others ran to find shelter under the dense canopy of a kurrajong tree where the ground was still dry. Of those who stayed out in the rain, one child reached out and ran her fingers along a cold steel rail to collect several drops before bringing them to her mouth to taste. Another turned his head to the sky, closed his eyes and poked out his tongue to catch as many drops as he could (Taylor & Rooney, 2016a). Rain and child bodies mingled and left traces on each other. We witnessed weather at work through the transcorporeality of skin and bodies as they met water.

In the next story we focus on the transcorporeal minglings of weather, air and smell; though it should be noted we are not suggesting a distinction between air and water despite their different matter, as air might be at once humid and thick with moisture or otherwise dry.

Dead fish

Children's curiosity about other creatures is no less so when they are dead. Dead creatures seem to be even more compelling. Next to the lake, we came across a scattering of large, rotting dead fish (see Figure 6.2). They looked like carp. Much discussion ensued about how they came to be there.

> *Children are keen to look, despite the stinky smell. Holding their noses to get as close as possible, they notice things — scales falling off the skin, exposed ribs and backbones.*
>
> > *"There's 4 dead fish. One, two, three, four."*
> > *"Eeewhh that fish is so yucky. I can smell it."*
> > *"Eewh. They are really stinky."*
> > *"What do you think made it dead?"*
> > *"It's a bit squashed."*
> > *"What do you think squashed it?"*
>
> *Some children see bugs crawling in the stomach remnants — which they refer to as "muck." One comments that another animal must have been eating the dead fish as half of their bodies are gone. "Someone ate it. Maybe a fox?" he suggests. Children are transfixed by the faces on the fish. Gaping mouths and prominent eyes give a foreboding look. A couple of children surmise from this that they are "bad fish" and this is why they are dead. They speculate that you can tell if they are good or bad fish "because of their mouths." They say "maybe this one's a good fish. Its mouth is like a good fish. It has a greedy smile (children laughing)." This explanation seems to resolve something about the scheme of life and death, at least in relation to dead fish found unexpectedly on a grassy shore.*
>
> *(Adapted from Taylor & Rooney, 2016b)*

FIGURE 6.2 Dead fish conversations

A week later, we visited the same place. The fish were still there. Decomposition had exposed more bones, the smell was gone and this time there was no talk of good or bad fish. Weathering exposure to sun and wind, fish skeletons and fishy atmospheres had changed. Children were curious about the changes, but no longer had the same visceral reaction.

Stumbling across a group of decomposing fish was unexpected. Face to face with the dead fish, children were drawn to speculating the fate of the fish through the remains of eyes and mouths. The wafting smell was potent. This was a situation where "one deep inhale [could] energise thinking, connecting noses with decay and other realities, possibilities and place" (Hennessy & Rooney, 2021, p. 10). The affects of airborne smells brought knowledge that was inhaled. The dead fish were not only inert figures on the ground, but they also created lively atmospheres in the aromas of decay. Carp is an invasive species that has become a pest causing widespread environmental damage in some of Australia's large river systems (Commonwealth Environment Water Office, 2016). Thus, in this encounter, we witness ordinary affects as political contact points. The colonial legacies that are bound up with introduced species such as carp, mean that just as the fish bodies lie exposed to the weather, so too does our own confusion about how to respond to death, decay and human-induced threats in complex ecological systems. Should we feel sorry for the fish and their fate? Or pleased that the lake's ecosystem has a few less invasive pests? Should we allow children to closely inspect the decay? Or move them on? The children seem able to stay with these types of contradictions exposed in the fish encounter; speculating as to what might be good, bad or neither. As Affrica Taylor (2019) notes in a similar scenario, when the children had to confront dead rabbits on some of our walks,

> [the children] seemed to be able to grasp and hold the deeply ecological understanding that all living beings are both dependent on and vulnerable to each other. In visceral and affective ways, they apprehend that we cannot be separated off – no matter how wild the invasive colonial legacies we are grappling with.
>
> (p. 116)

Our walks – and the unexpected yet everyday encounters these give rise to – thus provide an opportunity for young children to connect and know worlds differently. In this encounter, dead fish drew our sensory attention to the work of weather as a force of decay. We saw how heat, sun, wind and rain could alternately act as forces of both growth and decay over time (Hennessy & Rooney, 2021). Through first smell, and then the absence of smell, the children forged connections to creatures, earth, decomposing materials, compost, life, air and growth, and the work of weather. Children also came to know atmospheres as in part made up of smells that wafted through air and space in what might otherwise seem like a pleasant walk by a lake. Human bodies are breathing bodies that inhale what is in the air. Human comfort is not something to be taken for granted, and the messier aspects of clean air came to the fore in this encounter. What the children took from this into other experiences, such as air as carrier of pollution, mould or COVID (Tammi, 2019), is not clear. What is clear though is that this encounter was rich with "curiosity" and "impact" (Stewart, 2007) and that stumbling across the rotting fish was an opening for children to try to work out what was happening, how things had happened and what might happen next. Children experienced "the sensation that something is happening – something that needs attending to" (Stewart, 2007, p. 5), even if there was no clarity reached as to what this attention might look like.

Atmospheres of care

Thinking further with these two small weather stories, *Rain songs* and *Dead fish,* it becomes possible to see how atmospheres and affects matter in children's encounters with weather worlds. They also tell us something about the practice of care in context where climatic atmospheres are changing. There seems little doubt we need to find better ways to create atmospheres of care (and cared-for atmospheres) if human and more-than-human worlds are to respond, recuperate and live well together with climate change. We turn briefly to the question of what it means to *care* and how we understand children's sensory and

90 Relations: Weathering with more-than-human worlds

affective curiosity as a form care. This helps to explain why creating opportunities for these types of encounters is important in our feminist weather learning practice.

Traditionally the notion of care has often been romanticised as something we do for the good of others. Yet, it is also far more complex and contested. The act of caring can be a joy or a burden, and for the object of care it can feel good or it can oppress (Puig de la Bellacasa, 2017). In early childhood education, perhaps more so than any other professional field, the notion of care is also complex (see for example, Harwood et al., 2013; White & Gradovski, 2018). Despite this, there is still nonetheless a way in which care is important for both ethical practice and the creation of better worlds. Along with other scholars (Hodgins et al., 2019), we consider how we might extend our thinking beyond traditional, romanticised, obligated and unidirectional concepts of care by thinking with the work of María Puig de la Bellacasa and Donna Haraway in dialogue with children's affective encounters with weather.

Rain songs shows how rain, which makes puddles and changes how air feels and smells, does something to children's and Magpie's desires and bodies.[1] Although children were slightly interested in returning to the preschool, they were also keen to stay and play with rain and Magpie, stomping in puddles and catching raindrops. A satisfying sense of joyfulness was at work. Although playing in puddles might seem an odd encounter to discuss alongside the notion care, it is a deeply embodied and sensory meeting of child, water, Earth, Magpie and materials. Children showed an eagerness to connect with more-than-human companions and spent time getting to know the ways of water, testing out boundaries of comfort and discomfort, and inviting others into their play. We wonder what is happening in such encounters. How might children come to know weather worlds in such moments? Feminist thinking has drawn attention to the ways in which things can come to be known through bodies, touch and relations – knowledges that are often over-looked at the expense of the more dominant modes of knowledge gleaned through visual and therefore more distant or removed observation. Puig de la Bellacasa (2017) helps us to understand how touch, as a mode of connection, is worth considering more deeply insofar as it "embodies the involved intensities of caring doings and obligations" (p. 93). This is not to say that touch as a way of knowing is unproblematic, but rather that it is often neglected in knowledge making, and as Puig de la Bellacasa (2017) suggests, there may be a way of reclaiming this as a type of "caring knowing" (p. 98).

Dead fish was a less playful encounter, yet just as compelling. Children did not rush or turn away, but attended to the scattering of fish, noticing their presence and various stages of decay. They spent time with smells and weathered fishy atmospheres, as wafting affects invited a closer look. We think of this type of attention as an act of noticing small things that matter and that are connected to complex ecologies where humans are part of, not separate from, the worlds of fish. Children responded with curiosity in these and other encounters that accompanying adults had often brushed aside as too difficult or insignificant or unworthy of attention. We wondered if these moments of attentiveness demonstrated by children, might be something of what María Puig de la Bellacasa (2017) has in mind when she engages with the work of Donna Haraway in thinking about the politics of care. Puig de la Bellacasa (2017) observes that "Haraway has often called for engaged curiosity as a requisite of better caring for others in interspecies relations" (p. 92), and further that "care requires a form of knowledge and curiosity regarding the situated needs of an 'other' – human or not – that only becomes possible through being in relations that inevitably transform the entangled beings" (p. 90).

Atmospheric indicators provided one of the early insights into climate change, and the work of tracking the trajectory of climate change by the Intergovernmental Panel on Climate Change (https://www.ipcc.ch/) has in part looked to the degradation of Earth's unique life-sustaining atmosphere. Atmospheres engaged children on our walks with their life-giving potential. Raindrops are necessary for life; they feed the Magpie and plants. The smell of the decomposing fish was a strong reminder that something cyclical was happening. As the fish decomposed, its nutrients were soaking into Earth and the air that everyone was breathing. Fish air was making its way into us, into children, into plants, into Earth. It was everywhere and life giving. The smell and then the absence of the smell of the decomposing fish was an indicator that changes were occurring. Children attended to these atmospheres in ways that revealed potential for care and connection. None of these encounters were separable from the political atmospheres that surround climate change discourse. Just as rain and water are life giving, they can also overwhelm and destroy; as attested to by dramatic weather events such as floods and tsunamis, and slower happenings such as rising sea levels. Responsiveness and care (or lack of) is entangled in ethics, politics and the injustices of the uneven impacts of climate change on land and habitat devastation.

Conclusion

The multi-sensory dimensions of the *Rain songs* and *Dead fish* encounters show how atmospheric elements leave traces on and in bodies through both air and water. In such moments, children experience their bodies as "weather bodies" (Neimanis & Walker, 2014). They respond in various ways: singing, breathing, screwing up faces, laughing, imagining and questioning. These everyday moments invoke affective responses that suggest something is happening in children's bodily entanglements with the work of weathering (Pollitt et al., 2021). The unexpectedness of some encounters reminds us that we cannot really plan for or predict the weather affects that might draw us in as we walk along. Yet, at the same time, the openness and fluidity in children's sensory responsiveness to these weather encounters has helped us (as teachers and researchers) to recognise the importance of making such opportunities possible.

92 Relations: Weathering with more-than-human worlds

In this chapter, we have built further on the idea that feminist methods of sensory attunement to the elements can help in better understanding human relationship with wider climate worlds. Making time for practices such as these is not easy within an education framework dominated by outcomes and teaching facts about things – often conveyed through text, digital and visual media. We suggest however that we can only get closer to understanding the vitality and complexity of human-weather relations if children have opportunities for sensory and affective engagement with weather. The connections forged in small everyday encounters linger and move elsewhere via bodily traces of rain and inhaled atmospheres. It is these types of connections that open possibilities for care in responding to climate change.

Note

1 The Australian magpie (*Gymnorhina tibicen*) is a medium-sized black and white passerine bird native to Australia and southern New Guinea.

References

Alaimo, S. (2010). *Bodily natures: Science, environment, and the material self.* Indiana University Press.

Alaimo, S. (2016). *Exposed: Environmental politics & pleasures in posthuman times.* University of Minnesota Press.

Banerjee, B., & Blaise, M. (2013), There's something in the air: Becoming-with research practices. *Cultural Studies ↔ Critical Methodologies, 13*(4), 240–245. https://doi.org/10.1177/1532708613487867

Chen, M. Y. (2012). *Animacies: Biopolitics, racial mattering, and queer affect.* Duke University Press.

Clement, S. (2021). Walking with rain: Sensing family mobility on foot. In K. Barry, M. Borovnik, & T. Edensor (Eds.), *Weather: Spaces, mobilities and affects.* Routledge.

Clement, S., & Waitt, G. (2017). Walking, mothering and care: A sensory ethnography of journeying on-foot with children in Wollongong, Australia. *Gender, Place and Culture: A Journal of Feminist Geography, 24*(8), 1185–1203. https://doi.org/10.1080/0966369X.2017.1372376

Commonwealth Environment Water Office (2016) *Carp in the Murray-Darling Basin and Commonwealth environmental water.* https://www.awe.gov.au/water/cewo/carp-murray-darling-basin

Harwood, D., Klopper, A., Osanyin, A., & Vanderlee, M.-L. (2013). 'It's more than care': Early childhood educators' concepts of professionalism. *Early Years, 33*(1), 4–17. https://doi.org/10.1080/09575146.2012.667394

Flikke, R. (2019). Matters that matter: Air and atmosphere as material politics in South Africa. In P. Harvey, C. Krohn-Hansen & K. Nustad (Ed.), *Anthropos and the material* (pp. 179–195). Duke University Press. https://doi.org/10.1515/9781478003311-010

Gannon, S. (2016). Ordinary atmospheres and minor weather events. *Departures in Critical Qualitative Research, 5*(4), 79–90.

Grosz, E. (1994). *Volatile bodies: Toward a corporeal feminism.* Indiana University Press.

Hauge, B. (2013). The air from outside: Getting to know the world through air practices. *Journal of Material Culture, 18*(2), 171–187.

Hennessy, S., & Rooney, T. (2021). Watching change: Attuning to the tempo of decay with pumpkin, weather and young children. *Children's Geographies*, 1–14. https://doi.org/10.1080/14733285.2021.2007217

Hodgins, D., Yazbeck, S., & Wapenaar, K. (2019). Enacting twenty-first-century early childhood education: Curriculum as caring. In R. Langford (Ed.), *Theorizing feminist ethics of care in early childhood practice: Possibilities and dangers* (pp. 203–225). Bloomsbury.

Hohti, R., Rousell, D., MacLure, M., & Chalk, H.-L. (2021). Atmospheres of the Anthropocene. Sensing and rerouting dis/inheritances in a university museum with young people. *Children's Geographies*, 1–14. https://doi.org/10.1080/14733285.2021.1998369

Jackson, M., & Fannin, M. (2011). Letting geography fall where it may—Aerographies address the elemental. *Environment and Planning D: Society and Space*, *29*(3), 435–444.

Millei, Z., Korkiamäki, R., & Kaukko, M. (2019). Skates and skis. In P. Rautio & E. Stenvall (Eds), *Social, material and political constructs of arctic childhoods an everyday life perspective* (pp. 49–64). Springer. https://doi.org/10.1007/978-981-13-3161-9

Neimanis, A., & Walker, R. L. (2014). Weathering: Climate change and the 'thick time' of transcorporeality. *Hypatia*, *29*(3), 558–575. https://doi.org/10.1111/hypa.12064

Pollitt, J., Blaise, M., & Rooney, T. (2021). Weather bodies: Experimenting with dance improvisation in environmental education in the early years. *Environmental Education Research*, *27*(8), 1141–1151. https://doi.org/10.1080/13504622.2021.1926434

Pollitt, J., Blue, L., & Blaise, M. (2019). *Conversations with rain: A multi-platform research-creation project*. The Art Gallery of Western Australia. https://artgallery.wa.gov.au/learn/artist-activation/conversations-with-rain

Puig de la Bellacasa, M. (2017). *Matters of care: Speculative ethics in more than human worlds*. University of Minnesota Press.

Rooney, T. (2019b). Weathering time: Walking with young children in a changing climate. *Children's Geographies*, *17*(2), 177–189.

Rooney, T. (2019a). Sticking: The lively matter of playing with sticks. In D. Hodgins (Ed.), *Feminist post-qualitative research for 21st century childhoods* (pp. 43–51). Bloomsbury.

Rooney, T., Blaise, M., & Royds, F. (2019, April). *Manifesto: Weathering-with wind, shaping new pedagogies in times of climate change* [Conference presentation]. American Educational Research Association, Toronto, Canada.

Stewart, K. (2007) *Ordinary affects*. Duke University Press.

Tammi, T. (2019). Mold. In P. Rautio & E. Stenvall (Eds), *Social, material and political constructs of arctic childhoods an everyday life perspective* (pp. 17–34). Springer. https://doi.org/10.1007/978-981-13-3161-9

Taylor, A. (2019). Rabbiting: Troubling the legacies of invasion. In D. Hodgins (Ed.), *Feminist post-qualitative research for 21st century childhoods*. Bloomsbury.

Taylor, A., & Rooney, T. (2016a). Wet walking. *Walking with Wildlife in Wild Weather Times-A Common World Childhoods Research Collective Blog.* https://walkingwildlifewildweather.com/2016/05/30/wet-walking/

Taylor, A., & Rooney, T. (2016b). Rabbits in the grass and stinky fish. *Walking with Wildlife in Wild Weather Times-A Common World Childhoods Research Collective Blog.* https://walkingwildlifewildweather.com/2016/04/30/rabbits-in-the-grass-and-stinky-fish/

Vannini, P., Waskul, D., Gottschalk, S., & Ellis-Newstead, T. (2012). Making sense of the weather: Dwelling and weathering on Canada's rain coast. *Space and Culture*, *15*(4), 361–380. https://doi.org/10.1177%2F1206331211412269

White, E. J., & Gradovski, G. (2018). Untangling (some) philosophical knots concerning love and care in early childhood education. *International Journal of Early Years Education*, *26*(2), 201–211. https://doi.org/10.1080/09669760.2018.1458602

7

MULTI-SPECIES WEATHER ENCOUNTERS

Raindrops, mysteriously suspended, make visible a large spider web under the pine trees. Children are captivated by a golden orb-weaving spider in the centre of the web. It is at perfect eye-level and they spend time inspecting the spider's long stripy legs, the intricate forms of the web, and the strange leaf-like object trapped in it. The children are not sure if the spider is eating the trapped object or not.

(Adapted from Taylor & Rooney, 2017)

In this chapter, we explore the significance of children's relations with other species in shaping the ways children learn with weather and the ways they come to know weather worlds as shared or in common with multi-species others (Taylor & Pacini-Ketchabaw, 2019), including plants, animals, insects, other lifeforms and ecologies. As we observe children's relations, we also note how other species respond in the presence of children. Other creatures may not "care" about children's presence in the way we understand this term, but sometimes appear attentive through sounds, alert stillness or sudden movements.

In our research, it is children's encounters with other species that perhaps more than anything draws attention to both the mutual vitality and vulnerability of existence. Being out and about with children gives rise to possibilities for multi-species encounters and relations (Blaise, Hamm & Iorio, 2017; Taylor & Pacini-Ketchabaw, 2017). Through the lives of other creatures, children witness the work of weather in life, death, exposure to the elements, decay, decomposition and regeneration. On many of our walks, we stumble across the remains of dead creatures such as rabbits, possums and fish (see the dead fish encounter in the previous chapter). This is not to say we don't seek out creatures that are alive – we do! But many species are nocturnal, live underground or underwater, or in burrows, or fly high in the sky, or simply move too quickly for our capacity to notice. This is possibly why, when we see a dead

DOI: 10.4324/9781003150411-10

creature, the children stop and hang with it for a while, taking time to notice the remains of bones, scales, feathers, teeth and smells. Children also engage with the vitality and minutia of insect life through the rush of ants and bees. Bird life is abundant, as evidenced through the lively soundscape to our walks. Plants – as with the animals – are a mix of native and invasive species (such as blackberry bushes). They can be prickly, spiky or sticky, or soft and smooth. They can shade and shelter children, animals and earth from sun or rain, and they can fall and crash to the ground in winds and storms (see Rooney, 2019). As noted in the previous chapter, children's encounters with other species are far from straight-forward and raise complex conundrums and at times discomforting weather affects.

All living things – plants, fungi, animals, birds, insects, microbes and more – respond, grow and transform in relation to weather atmospheres and to each other. Many bee species, for example, live in collective colonies in which they work together to communicate, pollinate and contribute as part of larger interdependent ecosystems. Bees have symbiotic relationships with flowering plants that have been central to shaping the liveability of the world for human and more-than-human inhabitants (Nxumalo, 2018). Bees respond variously to warmth from the sun, oncoming storms or the presence of smoke, as well as to changing seasonal patterns that both impact and depend on bees to maintain rich biodiversity. Through relations such as these, the survival of bees and their multi-species companions, are linked to trajectories of climate change and weather (Soroye et al., 2020). In recent times, with the economic value of the agricultural industry under threat due to the decline of bee species, wider attention has been drawn to the ecological role and survival of bees (Calovi et al., 2021), highlighting both the interdependency and mutual vulnerability of humans and ecosystems. When children notice bees being busy in the sunshine or lingering with blossoms in springtime, they are not only witnessing the interconnectivity of weather, biodiversity and flourishing lives, they are also connecting with a diversity of life worlds who are weathering climate change together. In Fikile Nxumalo's (2018) work on children's encounters with dead and dying bees, she considers how we might pay attention to these changes; not just through emerging scientific knowledge on the decline of bee species, but also through children's everyday relations with the death of a bee. While such an encounter may seem minor in the scheme of a global climate (and bee) crisis, Nxumalo (2018) suggests that the opportunity to "learn to be affected by multiple forms of death" (p. 157) in the context of changing climate worlds, is also an opportunity to consider what it means to be responsible in such worlds.

In this chapter, we share a selection of stories of children's multi-species encounters, observing these through the weather worlds where we walk. Firstly, we tell of three starkly different animal encounters, involving a group of lively Eastern Water Dragons, a severed possum tail, and feathers moving with wind. Secondly, we turn to plant encounters, focusing on children's relations with the variety of grasses and the burnt remains of native grassland. As part of this we

96 Relations: Weathering with more-than-human worlds

share a reflection from the 2019–2020 Australian bushfires that devastated many plants and wildlife and yet also opened possibilities for regeneration.

In sharing these stories, we are interested in the children's responsiveness to multi-species weathering in complex climate worlds, noting that young children engage in ways that do not always fit the wider patterns of eco-grief or eco-anxiety that can accompany the rise in climate disasters and mass extinctions. We witness instead the curiosity and care with which children engage with weather, life, death and bushfire, and reflect on what this means for learning in contexts that will involve more frequent and confronting climate challenges. We also notice moments of recognition and mutual vulnerability between creatures; and suggest that it is through weather learning pedagogies and practice that this comes to the surface.

When working with children, one thing we note is the way they pay attention to the hidden or seemingly insignificant lives and activities of small or minor critters (Taylor, 2020). Children are quick to notice things that we (adults) might otherwise miss. Anna Tsing's (2015) work on the "arts of noticing" is important because it is how we are able to tell different kinds of stories, or as she puts it, "stories that we need to know" (p. 18). And for Tsing these are not just about disaster stories, but we also need to "… turn our attention to other sites of promise" (p. 18). The arts of noticing is grounded in the premise that the world is not just about or made by humans. Putting unpredictable encounters at the centre of things makes it possible to notice "patchy landscapes, multiple temporalities, and shifting assemblages of humans and nonhumans" (p. 20). Noticing other temporal patterns, such as Veronica Pacini-Ketchabaw and Kathleen Kummen (2016) do in regard to deer times and forest times, requires specific descriptions and imaginations. The arts of noticing is also about realising that we are surrounded by many world-making projects, but we might not yet know how to notice them. This will require experimentation, not knowing, failures, and lots of stumbling. This requires an open attitude and what Thom van Dooren, Eben Kirksey and Ursula Münster (2016) also call "passionate immersion," which can take many forms, but is about being attentive to the lifeways and experiential worlds of the more-than-human. Passion here is not about desire or love, but instead about becoming curious and learning how to be open to the unexpected and all the uncertainty that this might entail.

Creature encounters

In the three stories below, we share young children's encounters with some of earth's living creatures – reptiles, marsupials and birds. If we are to talk of climate change and children's encounters with the rich diversity of other living creatures, it would be remiss not to note that these stories are situated in a wider context of mass extinction.

The period in which we live, is overseeing unprecedented levels of extinction as a direct result of human activity and is said to be the sixth mass extinction

(Kolbert, 2014). While there are many factors that impact on extinction (such as habitat loss, drought or deforestation), anthropogenic climate change is one of the main drivers escalating this damage and the current wave of extinction. It is difficult to estimate the exact number of extinctions due to climate change, though studies suggest that as a direct result of human-induced climate change, the number is currently in the tens of thousands of species a year. Also, the exponential and sudden change in the rate of extinction is significant: "we are losing species at about 1000 times the rate at which new ones are evolving" (Raven, 2020, p. 11). This is a rate which had otherwise remained relatively steady for the 65 million years prior to our time, with the last mass extinction being the one that wiped out dinosaurs. Recent research on extinction, both in the sciences and humanities, warns that biological extinction is likely to be the most significant of all the damage that is being done to the living world and its ecosystems (Raven, 2020; van Dooren, 2014). As van Dooren (2014) suggests, "... in the future to come – if humanity is here at all – extinction will be among the handful of themes that is understood to be central, perhaps even definitive, of our time" (p. 5). Van Dooren (2014) goes on to note that we are currently witnessing the loss of substantial diversity of living forms across the planet, and that the lack of public attention to this tragedy seems to suggest that we still do not understand the significance of the interconnectedness of life in this world we share with other species. As a result, we are also missing the significance of this loss. Extinction is, to state the obvious, much more than the killing of an individual or group of animals. It "brings to an end whole ways of life" (van Dooren, 2014, p. 4); extinct species will never walk (or crawl or fly) on Earth again.

We have been deeply moved by the work by Thom van Dooren (2014), Deborah Bird Rose (2011) and the emerging field of extinction studies (i.e., Rose, van Dooren, Chrulew, 2017), whose scholarship tells of extinction through stories on the *unravelling* of ways of life and the loss that accompanies this. With Rose (2011), we want to think further about how we might bear witness to small parts of this unfolding disaster; for example, by witnessing changes to habitat and land, or the decline in creatures in places we return to over time. In our work with children, our regular practices of walking along, sensing and attuning seems to help engage children in the wider shared world – or perhaps more accurately, our practice of walking provides spaces and times where children might notice and respond to multi-species lives and worlds. These practices – for both research and pedagogy – can act as an antidote to the indifference that both Rose (2011) and van Dooren (2014) warn of; that is, they can offer young children a chance to recognise their own part in the connectivity, mutuality and diversity of all life forms.

Consistent with our approach throughout this book, thinking with weather offers a way to recognise and respond to the interconnectedness within multi-species encounters. In the three stories below, it is sun and warmth that draws water dragons out into the open to feed, it is rain and dampness that quickens the decay of the dead possum, and it is wind that moves children and feathers along

98 Relations: Weathering with more-than-human worlds

together. In these, and other ways, it is with weather that the children engage and connect with their multi-species companions.

Lively Eastern Water Dragons

> *Things are warming up. It's early summer and children linger by the lake in the shade. There's a splash in the shadows. A quick movement. Children return to dangling sticks in the water, making their own splashing sounds and watching ripples expand out across the lake. Conversations weave with water.*
>
> > *"I caught a fish. Everyone, look! A shoe."*
> > *"I found real seaweed. I caught real seaweed."*
> > *"Look, a plastic bag. Oh dear. A lot of rubbish in the water."*
> > *"I see ginormous mushrooms."*
> > *"Look at my feathers. I can make them like a rainbow."*
> > *"I see a duck."*
>
> *As ducks appear, children encourage quietness, "shh shh," while edging closer. In this still moment, the profile of an Eastern Water Dragon catches their attention. Head tilted and alert. Then they spot another and another. Five in all. This sighting is the first of its kind on our walks, and it's hard to tell who is more curious – water dragons or children.*
>
> *Children squat to have a closer look. It takes time for eyes to adjust to shades of grey and green, and striped tails that blend into the dappled shadows. A water dragon makes a sudden move. "It's eating a worm," says a child. Sure enough, we see a worm wiggling to free itself from the water dragon's mouth. Soon it is devoured. The reptile leaps into the lake. "It's swimming," says one child, who rushes along the lake keeping the water dragon in sight for as long as possible. "It's making ripples."*
>
> *After the walk, children tell their own stories of dragons, imagined and real. Stories that arise from, and yet exceed the immediacy of their water dragon encounter.*
>
> (T. Rooney, field note, 2017)

In this encounter, children have learned certain things about water dragons. For example, water dragons eat worms, they live on land and in water, they can swim and have skin that can camouflage into its surroundings. Weather learning takes this further, and invites the following kinds of questions: What weather entanglements do we notice as children meet water dragon? What might we see differently by observing this encounter as situated with the muddy bank, scattered litter, or overhanging trees? (see Figure 7.1). How might we foreground relations with air temperature, movement, sounds, colour and texture, time of day, shadows, and the Eastern Water Dragons? If we only stick to the facts extracted from the context, we might limit learning that could otherwise extend to notions of relationality, vulnerability and mutual curiosity, all of which connect the child to the worlds they share with these lively reptiles.

At the time of this encounter, it was warming up and damp edges of the lake offered a home for worms and a ripe feeding ground for water dragons. In

Multi-species weather encounters **99**

FIGURE 7.1 Eastern Water Dragon encounter

dappled shadows, reptiles sought shelter from predators. We could say they were weathering predation through the interplay and positioning of sun, warmth, skin, leaves, light and shadow. The presence of water dragons in this time and place was entangled with the possibilities and conditions of weather and seasonality. Children had been sharing this spot with the water dragons for some time, without being aware of their presence. The extended lingering by the lake – for both children and water dragons – was encouraged by clear skies and temperate conditions. On this occasion, it was a duck and the children's desire to see the duck more closely that, in stillness, alerted the children to the presence of the water dragons.

We wondered what else children noticed in this active ecosystem. There were so many small and seemingly unremarkable things and happenings we could comment on here; ripples, splashes, shadows, the inquisitive profile of water dragons, live worm eating, the stillness of curious crouching children, washed-up litter where the dragons were feeding, and much more. Through these multiple moments, we get a sense of how deeply weather is entangled in the possibilities of multi-species encounters and the emergence of relations between children, weather and other creatures. What children learn about and with water dragons cannot be extracted from the weather, and it is only by thinking with weather that we can see differently the ways children might forge relations and new understandings. A recognition of vulnerability was present, for example, in relation to worms as they were eaten, and water dragons as they scurried off to safety. Children were concerned that habitats and food might be vulnerable to the scattering of plastic litter. They wondered at the role of humans in this state of things. We witnessed acts of mutual respect and stillness. And all of this happened through a kind of "thrown-togetherness" (Massey, 2005) in a meeting of child, weather, creature, place and time (a theme we return to in the next chapter). A convergence of conditions offered a starting point for speculation on the lives of worms and dragons. New imaginings, a mixture of magical and real, emerged as children moved on from this encounter.

A severed possum tail

Lying on the ground is a single possum tail. For some time, a group of children stand around the tail, keeping slightly back as if not sure what to expect; some wonder if the tail might still be alive. One child says: "I think the front of it died. And the back is still alive." The tail remains still. Emboldened by its inertness, a child picks up a stick and prods it. Others caution: "It's a possum tail. Don't touch that. It could be a poison tail." Eventually, other children decide it might be safe, and one by one they set off in search of prodding sticks: "I'm going to find a stick. Me too." Using sticks, children reach out and gently poke the tail, checking for life and feeling its texture.

"It's not alive. It's fluffy."
"It might be a baby possum. Maybe this is the mummy of the baby."
"Just lift it. Don't be scared."
"Yuk. Yuk. Leave it there."
"There's something spiky on it. It's just the prickles."

The mood is sombre as we try to work out what might have befallen the possum. "Poor possum," children say.

One child recalls a skink that he had once seen lose its tail and explains: "When the tail came off it was moving and the lizard ran away." This prompts a more hopeful thought: "Maybe the tail came off the possum and the possum ran away."

Mystery far from solved, we head back to the preschool, leaving the tail to the whim of the elements.

(Adapted from Taylor & Rooney, 2017)

When we stumble across unexpected or curious sightings, we often stand back and watch the children, and only come closer if and when they call us. This story of children getting to know a severed possum tail was no exception. This was a chance meeting that we could not have envisaged or planned for in any pre-prepared environment lesson. This curious and somewhat confronting encounter instead provided an opening for talking, thinking and coming to know more about the tail as it lay exposed to the elements; weathering, decomposing and yet persisting in a state we could recognise. This is an example of

Multi-species weather encounters **101**

FIGURE 7.2 Reaching out to a possum tail

children learning with what was uncertain (was it alive or dead, safe or unsafe?), missing (literally in this case as the body of the possum was nowhere to be seen), unknown (what had happened to the possum?) and through seeking out connection. We noticed that sticks acted as conduits of connectivity, a phenomenon we have seen at other times on our walk and that we have come to understand as a practice of children "risking attachment" (Instone, 2015; Rooney, 2019). When children pick up sticks, they seem to use these as companions that extend their reach and help them to test the boundaries of their own vulnerability (see Figure 7.2).

As the sun glared down on the discarded tail, children were aware that the possum should be home in its bed. They know this because on another walk, we saw a possum out and about during the day making its way slowly through reeds by the lake. At first, they were excited, but this was soon dampened as they realised that the possum must be sick if it was out in the daytime. On that occasion, some children wondered if the possum was finding somewhere to die. In the story above, talk of death and dying are also prominent. Some children wondered if there was any sense in which the tail might still be alive, or even partly alive. Others sensed possible danger, suggesting caution as the tail could be poison. Children were neither comfortable nor uncomfortable with the notion of death, rather they were curious about what death might look like through

102 Relations: Weathering with more-than-human worlds

quite specific features noticed on the tail. The fluffiness suggested a fairly recent separation from the body, but spikiness and prickles already showed signs of the work of sun, wind and exposure. As children, tail and sunshine hovered in the presence of each other, one child remembered the familiar tale of how skinks escape their predators. This opened a glimmer of hope that perhaps somewhere out there was a possum without a tail, still living.

Ultimately, there were no answers to how or why the possum tail appeared as if from nowhere. We (adults) did not try to resolve the puzzle for the children, for we had no idea either. The children left, however, having reached out to something unusual and having witnessed a possum weathering their shared world. They moved on with the knowledge that the tail would continue in some way in their absence, though the exact process of change and decay with weather remained unknown. Children were far from indifferent in the way that van Dooren (2014) and Rose (2011) warn of, but did not simply mourn the possum either. They cared, connected and sought out the possibilities in which the possum tail might continue to have a presence in the world.

Feathers moving with wind

> *Children are collecting feathers today. They often do this on our walks; perhaps because of the softness, the colours, or simply the mystery of how they come to be on the ground. Children notice wind and feathers moving together.*
>
>> *"I like feathers. If you don't pick them up, they fly away."*
>> *"They have fluffy things and they're very soft."*
>> *"Feather... feather... feather! I got a baby feather, a mumma feather and a dadda feather!"*
>> *"I founded a feather. There's lots here. I founded double. It's tickling me!"*
>
> *Some children stop at every feather, gathering a small bundle to carry along.*
> *"That bird just dropped a feather." said a child. Moving between sunlight and shade, a child watches the colours on the feather change. "It's back on now. It's green. The shade makes it go off, and the sun makes it go on."*
>
> (F. Royds, field note, 2018, November 16)

This small story revealed insights into children's relations with wind, sun and shade through the playful activity of collecting feathers. We noted sensory connections, such as tickling, running after feathers in the wind, and the furry softness of feathers on skin (see Figure 7.3).

Feathers provided a different perspective to think with light, shade, colour, position and movement. One unexpected insight was that a child noticed the shifting sunlight in the changing colours of the feather. She talked about how sunlight and shadow somehow turned things *on* and *off*, and we were reminded that weather learning happens in many ways. In this case moving, positioning and repositioning feathers in light and shade was useful for coming to know feathers and something of the life of birds.

FIGURE 7.3 Gathering feathers

Conversations continued well after the feather encounter. Children wondered which birds the feathers came from and where the birds were now. Sometimes though, these types of musings came more at the prompting of adults present. Without thinking, we would find ourselves hurriedly trying to identify the species of bird (on our mobile phones!), so as to convey this important information to the children. As well as seeking out such details, we had to work hard to remind ourselves to also notice what it was about feathers that prompted children to reach out and carry them along. We continued to wonder in what ways these small affective, avian encounters might be bringing bird, child and weather together.

Plant encounters

The grassy woodland areas where we walked with children, lie between the Australian National University and a large lake. Patches of grassland stretch out between areas lightly treed with eucalypts, casuarinas and pine trees, and would once have been almost entirely kangaroo grass (Australian National University, 2012). Over time, the area covered by kangaroo grass has been reduced, firstly as a result of sheep grazing and then from increased urbanisation. The current grassed areas are thus a mix of curated lawn surrounding the university buildings, weeds and other introduced grasses, reeds by the lake and small patches of protected remnant kangaroo grass. Children would often return to favourite and familiar trees or patches of grass, even as these changed over the course of the year. They lay in grass, hugged the tree trunks and clambered through low branches to hide in the foliage. Some children planted seeds that they hoped would grow. On one walk, a child quietly placed a seed in the ground and covered it over, commenting "in 110 years it'll grow into a very big tree. It needs sunshine and water" (Rooney & Royds, 2018).

While there are many plant encounters we could share, we have chosen to tell two of children's encounters with grasses. Both in some ways talk to the continual shifts between flourishing, survival and destruction, and the connections between these happenings and the complexities of human–weather relations.

Soft grass, spiky grass, poison grass

We start our walk by taking time to lie on a patch of curated lawn. Children note the grass is "prickly," "furry" and "soft." Some children lie still with eyes closed. Others roll around or get up and try other spots. We walk on and children continue to sense grass on skin. Some say the tall kangaroo grass is scratchy on their legs. They reach out to test if the grass is spiky or soft, running their hands through stems and seeds, noticing different textures and feels.

Weed killer has been sprayed in one area to reduce the weeds. We warn children not to touch the pink patches of grass, because pink indicates poison. One child is fixated by the idea that people have intentionally poisoned the plants. She wants to know if we will get poisoned if we walk on the grass with our shoes on, or only with our shoes off. She wonders what will happen to animals that touch the poison grass, or the rabbits that eat the grass. Remembering the dead rabbits we have seen on earlier walks, she says "I think they might have died because they ate the poison grass." "I don't know why people poison the grass and kill the rabbits," she adds, struggling to make sense of such acts.

(Taylor & Rooney, 2016)

Once again, as with other stories we have told, we see children connecting with weather worlds through sensory curiosity. On every walk, these stretches of grass changed in colour, dryness, height and lushness. Changes in grass demanded our attention to shifts in weather and seasonality. During an extended period of drought, we noticed grassed areas become low, brown and sparse. Dust dominated the landscape and we wondered if grass would ever grow again. At other times, native grasses were dry, and yet tall and brimming with life and liveliness. In the warmer months, we avoided long grass as we knew snakes would be awakening, while in winter, the children would sit or lie for ages in the grass, playing or nesting or sometimes making things out of the long strands.

Above we also see how a child responded to the disconcerting details about poison. The concern over sprayed poison (a local land management practice to reduce the spread of weeds) showed children's engagement with the complex relations between human, environment and histories of the land. We understood that this practice aimed to protect the native grasslands and associated ecologies from invasive species that were continuing to take over the landscape. At the same time, it was understandable that the act of poisoning the grass would seem puzzling and counterintuitive to a child contemplating the flows and spread of poison. In thinking with the flows of poison spray, children understood the transcorporeality of air, land, water, plants, animals and their own clothing. In practice, wind and rain could result in runoff and airborne movement of poison particles, challenging the extent to which humans might contain and control the damage with this method of management (Hird, 2013).

Conversations such as these are one example of how we had to grapple with uncertainty and the challenges of containment that we witnessed on our walks. Although this learning environment was far from pristine or pure, there was much to offer in terms of learning that did not side-step the challenges of human intervention and entanglement. We wondered how encounters such as these might inform future conversations with children on invasive species, such as the need to cull cane toads, rabbits or the Snowy Mountain brumbies. All these result in contentious debate as the deliberate eradication of one species for the benefit of wider ecological survival can tug at human connections to life forms whose existence has been at various times been promoted, introduced and even romanticised (Taylor, 2013; 2019). Weather is one part of the conditions that allow a species to (unexpectedly, or at least unintentionally) thrive at the expense of other species. To grapple with these challenges is to learn with weather, and with the ongoing entanglement of humans and weather worlds.

Grass, fire and weather

In July 2019, we came across a large patch of grass burnt to the ground. Children stomped around and ash wafted from blackened clumps (see Figure 7.4). Small patches of smoke-like haze hung across the ground; while moisture in the air allowed the haze to hang and linger for a while. For just a moment, weather made visible the multiple and lingering effects of fire. This was a form of weather learning; though at the time, we had little sense that it would foreshadow a major bushfire season that brought widespread devastation to human and ecological communities.

> *Blackened earth. Charred by fire but not so hot as to decimate everything. Previously vibrant clumps of kangaroo grass are reduced to small tufts. Some show signs of regrowth only one week after the burn-off. Children stomp around and soon realise they can make smoke rise from the charred remains.*
>
> *"I think it's smoke" "It's blowing back"*
> *"The grass is black."*
> *"It's a control burn. It's where they burn down stuff."*
>
> *(T. Rooney, field note, July 2019)*

106 Relations: Weathering with more-than-human worlds

FIGURE 7.4 Making smoke

Some children take up Mindy's invitation to draw with ash in her notebook (see Figure 7.5).

> *Marks from a controlled grass fire in an Eastern state are made in a book already marked with rain from Western Australia. Weather mingling with children's markings. Small interactive acts of weather making show the relations between all things, coming together from other times, places and matters.*
>
> *(T. Rooney, field note, July 2019)*

We never found out if the burning of this piece of grassland was in preparation for a hot summer season ahead or part of a regular controlled management of the area, given that kangaroo grass flourishes in areas where low intensity fires occur periodically. Either way, already in winter, the possibility of bushfire had become a tangible and part of our weather conversations with the children. Little did we know that six months on from this encounter, the region would face some of its worst bushfires.

Tonya recorded the following short story in the midst of the bushfires in Eastern Australian during 2019–2020; the fires that emerged in the summer months after the children's encounter with the burnt grasslands. The story does not do justice to the devastation to wildlife, land and humans that occurred

FIGURE 7.5 Marks of rain and fire

during that time; but does speculate on how such events might lead us to reimagine the relationship between humans, weather, climate and responsibility.

> *It is November 2019. Fires have been lit by a lightning strike in the nearby mountains. Charred eucalypt leaves lie scattered over the lawn, brought on by the wind. One small sign of a fire many kilometres away. Wind, air, storms and fire are moving together, though at this stage there is little sense of just how entangled they will become. As the bushfires escalate, so does the urgency of warnings coming via apps and weather reports. With hundreds of separate fires burning out of control, the weather reports no longer headline sunshine, wind and rain. Instead, they report air quality index figures and point to moving patches of smoke, not rain clouds, on national and global satellite images. We are learning a new language – fire tornadoes, pyrocumulonimbus clouds, and bushfire thunderstorms. The fires are no longer viewed as a phenomenon external to other weather events; for example, started by lightning, flamed by winds or simply waiting for rain to put them out. The fires have become weather. From my garden, I now understand that the fluffy white clouds set against the bright blue sky are no ordinary clouds. They are pyrocumulonimbus formations rising from a bushfire just over the hill, generated by hot air rising from the fire and the moisture in the air, perhaps exacerbated by the water bombing from helicopters whirring overhead.*

108 Relations: Weathering with more-than-human worlds

> *In January, visiting one site of the fire a few weeks later, and walking down once familiar paths in the burnt out landscape, I feel seen; exposed for the thoughtlessness of human activity over time that has somehow converged here, escalating the scale and ferocity of the fires. No sign of life anywhere, and once vibrant bird life is barely a tinkle. I find out later, it is estimated that billions of animals and birds perished in the Australian fires, with entire species likely lost; gone, extinct. In these burnt spaces, weather and fire forge new relations. Fire can decimate a landscape, yet in the right conditions, it can also trigger germination and regrowth. The seeds of some native Australian plants do not just respond to rain and sunshine, but to fire, heat, ash in the soil and smoke. Each of these elements become weather conditions that release and nurture new plant growth after the fires. Through these processes of regeneration, we also witness fire as weather.*
>
> *(Rooney, 2020).*

During the bushfires, conversations seemed to pull notions of fire and weather closer together. It was all anyone could think and talk about. We came to know the weather as more complex. Not something that simply appears from the sky, but something more deeply embedded in the interconnectivity of Earth, plants and living creatures. As Tonya also reflected:

> *Breathing in smoke from the fires, I became conscious that the thick airborne ash consists of a mix of charred earth, vegetation, wildlife and other materials, all decimated in the path of fire. I walk and breathe. I too am earth.*
>
> *(Rooney, 2021)*

Bushfires can lead us to think differently about human-weather relations. As shown above, even the idea of *weather* itself was challenged and reconceptualised. What we thought of as cloud cover or atmosphere was similarly reconfigured in face of unfamiliar bodies of swirling ash, moisture, heat and air. Research has shown that as the intensity and frequency of bushfires grows, the chances of ecosystem regeneration are reduced (Gallagher et al., 2021). With this comes a further responsibility to think about how we respond to fires and care for earth in-between fire events. The 2019–2020 bushfires in Australia, drew increased attention to the value of Indigenous fire management practices to work with land and weather, seeking balance and regeneration through deliberate frequent low-intensity fire lighting. These are important practices that can stem both the destruction of ecological landscapes and the extinction of vulnerable species (Bird et al., 2018).

The notion of bushfire weather – that is, understanding bushfires *as* weather – can help to highlight how our (human) responsibility to the environment is not only to plants, animals and ecosystems, but also to atmospheres, cloud formations, moisture, air and everything that make up the atmospheric conditions we and others inhabit.

Conclusion

While we discussed plant and animal encounters separately above, we acknowledge that these are inseparable parts of the ecologies, ecosystems, atmospheres and climate systems within the weather worlds we walk through with children. The multi-species weather encounters described are not necessarily unique; they are a few of any multitude of unexpected encounters that could occur on any day out walking, or that could arise over any season or year as climate patterns become increasingly erratic and unstable. What matters is how we think about these encounters and recognise them as opportunities to grapple with the pedagogical and ethical dimensions of minor and ordinary happenings within extraordinary weather worlds. In acknowledging the many diverse and multi-species inhabitants in a particular place, Iris Duhn (2017) reminds us that the key question is "how can we learn to make spaces for living well, and sustainably, together with humans, more-than-humans, and vibrant matter of all kinds." (p. 45).

As noted above, there was a period when many of our walks with children occurred during months of drought. Over this time, we noticed children making their own dust storms and smoke clouds. On other walks, they were sometimes koalas clinging to trees as if their lives depended on it and they played with their shadows in the glare of the blazing sun. These children have not just lived with weather. They made weather, played with weather, sang with weather and weathered weather together. We understand these actions as form of responsiveness to the weather worlds we walk through, and a way in which children take time to be curious about the times and lives of multi-species companions.

References

Australian National University. (2012). *ANU heritage study Acton campus - Volume 1: Heritage study. Godden Mackay Logan Pty Ltd.* https://services.anu.edu.au/files/document-collection/Volume_1_of_the_ANU_Acton_Campus_Heritage_Study.compressed.pdf

Bird, R. B., Bird, D. W., Fernandez, L. E., Taylor, N., Taylor, W., & Nimmo, D. (2018) Aboriginal burning promotes fine-scale pyrodiversity and native predators in Australia's Western Desert. *Biological Conservation, 219*, 110–118. https://doi.org/10.1016/j.biocon.2018.01.008.

Blaise, M., Hamm, C., & Iorio, J. M. (2017). Modest witness(ing) and lively stories: Paying attention to matters of concern in early childhood. *Pedagogy, Culture and Society, 25*(1), 31–42. https://doi.org/10.1080/14681366.2016.1208265

Calovi, M., Grozinger, C. M., Miller, D. A., & Goslee, S. C. (2021). Summer weather conditions influence winter survival of honey bees (Apis mellifera) in the northeastern United States. *Scientific Reports, 11*(1), 1–12. https://doi.org/10.1038/s41598-021-81051-8

Duhn, I. (2017). Cosmopolitics of place: Towards urban multispecies living in precarious times. In K. Malone, T. Gray, & S. Truong (Eds.), *Reimagining sustainability in precarious times* (1st ed., pp. 45–57). Springer. https://doi.org/10.1007/978-981-10-2550-1_4

110 Relations: Weathering with more-than-human worlds

Gallagher, R. V., Allen, S., & Mackenzie, B., et al. (2021). High fire frequency and the impact of the 2019–2020 megafires on Australian plant diversity. *Diversity & Distributions, 27*, 1166–1179. https://doi.org/10.1111/ddi.13265

Hird, M. J. (2013). Waste, landfills, and an environmental ethic of vulnerability. *Ethics and the Environment, 18*(1), 105–124. https://doi.org/10.2979/ethicsenviro.18.1.105

Instone, L. (2015). Risking attachment in the Anthropocene. In K. Gibson, D. B. Rose, & R. Fincher (Eds.), *Manifesto for living in the Anthropocene* (pp. 29–36). Punctum Books.

Kolbert, E. (2014). *The sixth extinction: An unnatural history*. Holt.

Massey, D. (2005). *For space*. SAGE Publishing.

Nxumalo, F. (2018). Stories for living on a damaged planet: Environmental education in a preschool classroom. *Journal of Early Childhood Research, 16*(2), 148–159. https://doi.org/10.1177/1476718X17715499

Pacini-Ketchabaw, V., & Kummen, K. (2016). Shifting temporal frames in children's common worlds in the Anthropocene. *Contemporary Issues in Early Childhood, 17*(4), 431–441. https://doi.org/10.1177/1463949116677930

Raven, P. H. (2020). Biological extinction and climate change. In W. K. Al-Delaimy, V. Ramanathan, & M. S. Sorondo (Eds.), *Health of people, health of planet and our responsibility: Climate change, air pollution and health* (pp. 11–20). Springer.

Rooney, T. (2019). Sticking: The lively matter of playing with sticks. In D. Hodgins (Ed.), *Feminist post-qualitative research for 21st century childhoods* (pp. 43–51). Bloomsbury.

Rooney, T. (2020, December). *Weather wonderings* [Workshop]. Weathered Lives, Durham University UK. https://weatheredlives.org.uk/event/weather-wonderings/

Rooney, T. (2021). Moved by wind and storms – Imaginings in a changing landscape. In K. Barry, M. Borovnik, & T. Edensor (Eds.), *Weather: Spaces, mobilities and affects*, (pp. 38–50). Routledge.

Rooney, T., & Royds, F. (2018, August). Digging, dissolving dirt. *Weathering Exploring climate change pedagogies with children*. https://weathercollaboratory.blog/2018/08/30/digging-and-dissolving-dirt/

Rose, D. B. (2011). *Wild dog dreaming: Love and extinction*. University of Virginia Press.

Rose, D. B., van Dooren, T., & Chrulew, M. (2017). *Extinction studies: Stories of time, death, and generations*. Columbia University Press.

Soroye, P., Newbold, T., & Kerr, J. (2020). Climate change contributes to widespread declines among bumble bees across continents. *Science, 367*(6478), 685–688. https://doi.org/10.1126/science.aax8591

Taylor, A. (2013). *Reconfiguring the natures of childhood*. Routledge.

Taylor, A. (2019). Rabbiting: Troubling the legacies of invasion. In D. Hodgins (Ed.), *Feminist post-qualitative research for 21st century childhoods* (pp. 111–118). Bloomsbury.

Taylor, A. (2020). Countering the conceits of the Anthropos: Scaling down and researching with minor players. *Discourse: Studies in the Cultural Politics of Education, 41*(3), 340–358. https://doi.org/10.1080/01596306.2019.1583822

Taylor, A., & Pacini-Ketchabaw, V. (2017). Kids, raccoons, and roos: Awkward encounters and mixed affects. *Children's Geographies, 15*(2), 131–145. https://doi.org/10.1080/14733285.2016.1199849

Taylor, A., & Pacini-Ketchabaw, V. (2019). *The common worlds of children and animals*. Routledge. https://doi.org/10.4324/9781315670010

Taylor, A., & Rooney, T. (2016, November, 20). Another grassy walk. *Walking with Wildlife in Wild Weather Times-A Common World Childhoods Research Collective Blog*. https://walkingwildlifewildweather.com/2016/11/20/another-grassy-walk/

Taylor, A., & Rooney, T. (2017, June 8). Bones, teeth, claws and tails. *Walking with Wildlife in Wild Weather Times-A Common World Childhoods Research Collective Blog*. https://walkingwildlifewildweather.com/2017/07/19/bones-teeth-claws-and-tails/

Taylor, A., & Rooney, T. (2017, March 21). The difference weather makes. *Walking with Wildlife in Wild Weather Times-A Common World Childhoods Research Collective Blog.* https://walkingwildlifewildweather.com/2017/03/21/the-difference-weather-makes/

Tsing, A. L. (2015). *The mushroom at the end of the world: On the possibility of life in capitalist ruins.* Princeton University Press.

van Dooren, T. (2014). *Flight ways: Life and loss at the edge of extinction.* Columbia University Press.

van Dooren, T., Kirksey, E., & Münster, U. (2016). Multispecies studies: Cultivating arts of attentiveness. *Environmental Humanities, 8*(1), 1–23.

van Doreen, T., Rose, D. B., & Chrulew, M. (2017). Extinction studies: Stories of time, death and generations. Columbia University Press.

8
EARTH AND DEEP WEATHER TIMES

Several eroded channels now run through one of our lakeside hang outs. Recent rain has gouged out mud; a reminder that land is never still. Children leap and sidestep across the uneven surface as they navigate the new terrain. A few bend to explore trickling rivulets that continue to carve and shape the earth. One child picks up a clump of dirt. Taking care to keep it whole, he places it in the lake and watches it dissolve. Earth bubbles. Particles of dirt seem to come alive as they separate and dissipate, making a murky patch in otherwise clear water. A lively weathered exchange of water, air and mud makes new earthy trails.

(T. Rooney, field note, 30 August 2018)

The layers of earth and rock tell much of the times in which we live. We are now in the age of the Anthropocene (Steffen et al., 2018), where the presence of humans on Earth will at some point be reduced to geological layers of plastic and other waste with decomposition timeframes that will outlive our own time. These layers will reveal the practices of production and consumption that dominated the last years of many humans on Earth, and perhaps, along with human fossils, may also lie the last fossils of many millions of other species that became extinct due to human disregard for the lives and earth that sustained us. Of course, this scenario is not yet set in stone (so to speak), but neither is it out of the question. And this is not just a future concern, for the slow weathering of waste materials and the Earth's weathering of our human presence is happening here and now. The worlds we choose to make with weather and Earth might shift this trajectory, as many worlds are possible. As argued throughout this book, an understanding of human-weather relations is one perspective through which we might (re)frame human responses to environmental challenges, and here we look at this notion through the lens of Earth and time.

DOI: 10.4324/9781003150411-11

FIGURE 8.1 Everything is moving. Always

Ever-changing patterns in the shifting and shaping of planet Earth lie in the deep time of rocks and geologies. It may seem obvious that the places where we live and walk are shaped by ongoing weathered histories; from a simple rain shower, to deluges and landslides, to earthquakes and glacier movements as well as the longer-term shifts in tectonic plates. There is little stillness. Everything is moving. Always (see Figure 8.1).

In the context of the Anthropocene, we are also aware of the impact humans have on the formation and movement of the geological layers and features of Earth. What is less obvious is the relationship between humans and the rocky layers of earth that stretch way back before we (humans) were even on Earth. These deep geologies are however much more entwined with our human lives than we might think. In this chapter we examine and challenge some commonly held views on the relationships between: human agency and earth; notions of past, present and future; and living and non-living entities. In doing so, we draw attention to the histories and futures that frame the current climate crisis and the pedagogical potential of attuning more closely to weather times and places in environmental education. We draw on the work of writers such as Elizabeth Povinelli, Kathryn Yusoff, Doreen Massey, and the Bawaka collective, all of whom in some way challenge us to think differently about the interconnections between rocks, soil, time and weather conditions such as rain or fog. We reflect

The geology of human agency – Rocks, soils and minerals

Kathryn Yusoff draws our attention to the significance of rocks and minerals in the context of responding to climate change, and in particular the deep geological histories of earth. Yusoff (2013) says that "a deep history of geologic life might well elaborate on more generative climate futures ... and offer alternative imaginaries for the inhuman forces within humanity" (p. 781). Yusoff (2015) argues that humans are in part constituted by non-local, geological forces through the ways these bring possibilities for "entities to be what they are" (p. 384). That is, there are inhuman, deeper geological forces from other times and places that are somehow part of what we are in the here and now. These are what Yusoff refers to as the "mineralogical dimensions of humanity" (p. 384). Yusoff is not suggesting we think of ourselves as a simple hybrid of human/nonhuman elements that are somehow stuck together, but rather that this boundary does not make sense if we understand the inhuman as entangled "within the very composition of the human" (p. 384). As Yusoff points out, it is common to acknowledge biological forces as the foundation of life and change. She goes on to argue that this is not the full picture and that we need to add to this an acknowledgement of geology in the formation of the subject.

In thinking with the deeper geological times of earth and rocks, and the ways these have a presence in our own life and time on Earth, we can also turn to the topmost geological layer via current discussions and concerns in relation to earth as soil. Stretching across all aspects of ecological and environmental care, debates about the fertility and depletion of soil have given rise to a renewed focus on soil science and soil care. We see in this debate a familiar pattern, whereby the urgencies in the soil debate have been pushed along by a need to address the implications for (human) food security, but ultimately also draw attention to the significance of the relationship between humans, plants, earth, micro-matter, insects, weather, water and the rich interconnectivity of human and more-than-human worlds that remain crucial to healthy soil. Recognising human neglect of soil care in some farming and extraction practices, draws attention back to the fact that we can no longer ignore that we (humans) are part of the very environment that we have damaged over time. Response and recuperation are needed, and this can be informed by an understanding of soil-human relations. In the vein of our investigation here, we draw attention to the work of the weather in shaping these relations. In our field work, we have noticed the ways children recognise the circulation of earth and matter, such as when they reflected on ants as both earth movers and composters. Ants may seem small and insignificant, but it is worth observing that "[t]heir work in composting the earth to make it viable for other life forms not only predates our own relatively short, if spectacular, human life on earth, but will most likely postdate us as well." (Taylor & Pacini-Ketchabaw, 2015, pp. 512–513).

Earth and deep weather times **115**

FIGURE 8.2 Making a dust storm

By focusing on child-weather relations, we have come to recognise the weathering of geologies in the ongoing shifting and shaping of children with earth. We notice that rocks, sand, and the composing and decomposing of earthy matter feature often in children's encounters with place. The following story tells of co-making with wind, dust and storms (also see Figure 8.2).

> *Widespread drought conditions offer context for the dry and denuded landscape we wander through on this wintery walk. Warm coats hug our bodies. Earth is partly covered in tufts of dry grass and scatterings of bark, over what is otherwise an expanse of soft yellow dust. In low shady areas, green glints of moss are visible; a sign that this diverse lakeside environment still holds moisture in hidden places. Children reach down and feel the softness of dust. Some stomp dirt to break down the harder clumps, and step back to witness disintegration and the imprint of shoes on dry earth. They squash clumps, explaining "it becomes dirt." Scratching at the ground, children let earth run through their fingers. One slowly releases crushed dirt from a standing height – a mini dust storm ensues.*
>
> *(Rooney & Royds, 2018)*

These intimate exchanges between child, earth and water, make visible the ways that humans too are part of the constant shifting and shaping of geological

116 Relations: Weathering with more-than-human worlds

matter (see also Rooney, 2021a). In small moments such as these, we wonder how children experience their own entanglement in the circulation of earthy materials and rocky histories that stretch long before the times of these encounters, and yet also reach into our daily concerns and cares.

Weather times – Past, present and future

Thinking with how Earth's deeper histories may manifest in our bodies and lives requires us to consider the relationship between past, present and future. In the context of the challenges of climate change, time is said to be of the essence, and yet is also in many ways illusive.

In her paper, *Weathering Time*, Rooney (2019) sets out some initial explorations into the diverse, non-linear and overlapping temporalities that run through weather worlds, challenging our narrow perceptions of temporality as linear and singular. In this section, we take up this theme and consider how we might conceptualise the relationship between past, present and future through the complex relations that shape Earth, weather, climate and possible futures. In the context of climate change, where human-induced damage has resulted from progress driven activity that continues to push forward regardless of the cost to Earth, how we orient ourselves towards the future seems important. The temporality underlying capitalist activity is arguably linear, fast-paced, often mechanised and directed towards the benefit of some humans, and at the expense of others and more-than-human worlds. Rethinking temporality is one way to attend to the times of Earth, weather, climate and the deeper times in the lived worlds of all beings. Jacob Metcalf and Thom van Dooren (2012) suggest that one way to acknowledge temporal diversity in the context of environmental change, is to think and imagine with "more-than-human" times and scales and to note that we cannot "assume that all temporalities are identical, let alone synchronous" (p. viii). Here, we turn to the relationship between weather and time, to consider how this might shed light on more diverse temporalities.

In human experience, there is a certain familiarity in attuning to the relationship between weather and time. Installation artist, Olafur Eliasson (2003), explains how through our human relationship with weather "(w)e have learned to use and relate to weather as a mode of time. The weather helps us to get our heads around the abstract notion of what time is, making it more tangible" (p. 132). This happens through the shifts in temperature during the day, or seasonal changes that become part of our lived experience. With Astrida Neimanis and Rachel Walker (2014), rather than seeing weather events as occurring *through* time as a separable domain, we consider in what sense we might understand weather *as* time or time *as* weathering.

To expand on this, and thinking with Doreen Massey (2006), our aim is to shift the perception of time as the dominant driving force underpinning change, and to articulate a more entangled view of the activity between time, place, matter and being. To do so, we consider alternative views on the relationship

Earth and deep weather times **117**

between time and place. According to Massey (2006), engaging with the temporality of place can provide an opening to knowledges and imaginations that lie beyond the immediacy of our experience. Thinking with temporalities of place allows us to rethink the common positioning of time as the dominant dimension of change (also see Massey, 2005) and on this view, landscape is seen as more than a stable surface upon which changes occur over time, and rather *is* the "movement of the rocks" that can be "imagined as provisionally intertwined simultaneities of ongoing, unfinished stories" (Massey, 2006, p. 46). This more entangled view of time and space can help us to imagine something more lively than what we commonly think of as a singular *here and now* in a certain place and time. Add to this the idea that we can think of weather as not only a causal force, but rather something more akin to weather *as* time and *as* change in rocks and earth, and it becomes possible to conceptualise a more complex and inseparable notion of time-place-weather.

To briefly return to the work of Povinelli (2016), one curious idea in her view of the future is that:

> *The future depends on the kinds of connections that are made in, and made possible by, the world that exists and the differential forces that keep it in place or move it. That is, the future is not a place somewhere or sometime else.*
>
> *(Povinelli, 2016, p. 115)*

The notion that the future is not a place somewhere or sometime else is challenging. How else might we conceptualise notions of change over time or the direction toward which such change is oriented? Povinelli seems to be suggesting that what matters is the constant shifting and shaping in the world as it exists. When Povinelli talks about the changes in fog (for example, when with pollution or smoke it becomes smog), she notes that this is not a sudden catastrophic change but rather multiple changes that "accumulate in a series of condensed and coordinated quasi-events" (p. 113). It is these small events that Povinelli says are the basis of change and existence. And so, rather than look to the future as the time and direction of change – we are invited to focus on what is happening in the "hereish" and "nowish." This alternative articulation to the usual *here* and *now* captures the idea that every place and time we find ourselves is far from singular, and rather always consists of times and places that we may not immediately recognise as manifesting themselves in that moment. "Hereish" and "nowish" also create a little bit of uncertainty and make room for all sorts of weatherings to blur, mix-up, and accumulate. A more rigid notion of the present understood strictly as *here and now* immediately draws attention to borders between events and objects – rather than on the forces of endurance and relations. A similar thickening of what we understand as the present is also presented in the work of Donna Haraway and (albeit in a different way) Doreen Massey.

Haraway (2016), for example, also eschews futurism, instead focusing on the multi-species collaborations and combinations needed to *become-with* each other

118 Relations: Weathering with more-than-human worlds

in what she conceives of as the *thick* present. As she says: "I try to cultivate a way of thinking that is not futurist but rather thinks of the present as a thick, complex tangle of times and places in which cultivating response-abilities, capacities to respond, matters" (cited in Mitman, 2019, p. 17). In reflecting on the work of Deborah Bird Rose with Australian Aboriginal people, Haraway suggests that the kind of present that involves being serious about taking care of Country is "not instantaneous but thick" (cited in Mitman, 2019, p. 20). This is reflected in our reading of the work of the Bawaka collective, who also share ideas on the relationality and connectedness of weather, place and time:

> For Yolŋu, this walking is time. Time is attending to Country, being Country, feeling Country, living relationships. It is the getting of bush foods, the gathering of oysters and larani, bush apple. It is the checking for bush foods and the knowing, the feeling when they are ripe and ready, the joy, the touch of the ground, the sweat. Time is relationships with and as Country. And in this walking and checking and gathering, in these relationships, the beings and becomings of weather are active co-constituents. Weather is a lively presence, a source of information and temporal marking. It enrolls the beings and becomings of Country in a shared language or dharuk communicated through intimate, entangled relationships between people, processes, affects and things.
>
> (Bawaka Country et al., 2020, p. 298)

Actions that we might often think of as *in the present* are therefore much more complex and bound up in multiple trajectories of becomings, gatherings, histories, weathers and geologies, that, according to Doreen Massey, we can only recognise as *here* and *now* (or following Povinelli, "hereish" and "nowish") because there is an "outrageous specialness of the current conjunction" at this moment and in this place (Massey, 2005, p. 42). With this recognition comes responsibility:

> The past is hurt by the present. We are also hurting the ancestors from the future now. This means that while thinking of "future generations" is important in bringing the realities of change alive, our children's children are not separated from us by a gulf of time. Rather, they live now, already, in our bodies and through their active presence in this world.
>
> (Bawaka Country et al., 2020, p. 299)

Thus, there is no singularity in time and place that we can easily locate as past, present or future, nor is there a linear, forward trajectory of change. Rather, what matters is the *ongoingness* of space, time and earthly inhabitants and the responsibility that we take for this in the *thick* present of our times on earth. As Haraway says, ongoingness can be thought of as the "nurturing, or inventing, or discovering, or somehow cobbling together ways for living and dying well with each other in the tissues of an earth whose very habitability is threatened"

(Haraway, 2016, p. 132). In our work with weather, we think of weathering together with time and place as inseparable from the ongoingness of space and time (Neimanis & Walker, 2014; Rooney, 2019).

When Metcalf and van Dooren (2012) invite us to attune more closely to the temporal diversity beyond our limited human notion of linear, clock time, we can turn to more-than-human worlds, weather worlds and the traces of other lifetimes that lie deep in the earth. This is however not easy work. Returning again to the Bawaka collective we are reminded,

> (h)uman perception cannot even start to comprehend many of the complex temporalities at work here. For by attending to more-than-human agencies of time and weather, diverse multiplicities emerge even as they are beyond human understanding. This is the seasonal time of clouds gathering. It is also the time of hydrological cycles, of water moving through aquifers for thousands of years, of transpiration and growth. And short spirals, of the flash of lightning, claps of thunder, of traveling sound and light. There is neither a single weather, nor a single time, nor an inherent difference between time and matter and embodied experience, affect and the beings and becomings of Country.
> (Bawaka Country et al., 2020, p. 300)

What we can take from this work is that, despite these conceptual challenges, we need to look beyond our ingrained perception of routine and day-to-day life to understand time as neither abstract nor separable from our presence in the world. Our relationships with weather worlds are also relationships with time and with change, and this is significant if we are to connect more closely with the shifting and shaping of climate change. That is:

> the co-emergence of people with each other and with weather and time speaks to a need to understand and attend to the weather and climate as us, to respond as weather rather than to it. Climate change is never over there or simply in the future.
> (Bawaka Country et al., 2020, p. 301) [Italics in original]

In our work, we notice children reflect on wider geological scales and times (Rooney, 2019), with musings ranging from meteors to monsters to dinosaurs. We listen, and as the following excerpt shows, their conversations carry on, weaving through leaps and connections over time and place:

> "Look. Dinosaur bones."
> "We always find dinosaur bones here don't we?"
> "They died because a meteor hit the earth."
> "Big meteor hit the earth, then it got all the dinosaurs."
> "Or it might have been a snowstorm."
> "They killed each other."
> (all singing) "Dinosaur bones … … dinosaur bones… dinosaur bones…. I found two dinosaur bones"
>
> (F. Royds, field note, 2 November, 2018)

120 Relations: Weathering with more-than-human worlds

As we witness the imaginative leaps that children make between now and then, or the now-ish and then-ish, we notice a blurring of these boundaries in ways that reveal a more fluid notion of time and place than the one they experience in the daily routines of preschool life. In her writing on weather worlds in outer space, Kimberley Peters (2021) talks of the sound of wind blowing on Mars, noting that it is more recognisable than we might think. Perhaps the children's speculations of other worlds and times, isn't so crazy after all and is in fact a way of making important connections with other times, places and worlds.

Living and non-living entities – Fog, smog and pollution

Another concept that is often taught as a foundational education concept is the notion that there is a distinction between living and non-living. Indeed, assessments of children's capacity and developmental progress often include tests on the extent to which they can accurately identify things as either living or non-living. While such processes can provide insights, they can also perpetuate a framing of life/non-life as a foundational category of knowledge, without leaving room for a child's more curious questioning about these notions (Merewether, 2020). Answers are presented as binary choices, rather than allowing children to sit with more complex ideas such as "is my computer alive?". Beyond the classroom, the framing of a clear boundary between life/non-life has met with critique and is far from certain. Mel Chen's (2012) work on animacies for example seeks to "trouble the binary of life and nonlife as it offers a different way to conceive of relationality and intersubjective exchange" (p. 11). As discussed below, in the context of climate change, the distinction has come under even greater scrutiny in ways that should challenge us (humans) to carefully rethink human-world relations, and the nature of what is lively and in existence.

To return to Yusoff, if as she suggests, our living bodies are also in part mineralogical and geological, we have to ask what sense does it make sense to try to separate out or draw boundaries around what is living or non-living in our world? This question is significant, as constructing such a distinction can lead to hierarchies and structures where the living is valued over the non-living in ways that arguably ignore the liveliness and vitality of many things that exist in our world, or worse, that justify the ongoing destruction of much that is seen as non-living. If we are to approach environmental education in a way that acknowledges interconnectivity and relationality, then it is worth considering the implications of how we frame and discuss all that exists with a more fluid and sceptical approach to boundaries.

In Elizabeth Povinelli's work *Geontologies: A Requiem to Late Liberalism* (2016), she exposes the problems inherent in the tendency to think of existence through the distinction between life and non-life. Povinelli (2016) explains that so often, this distinction is used to underpin certain actions, policies or ideas that end up justifying exploitation and dominance of "life" over "non-life"; for example, to justify the extraction of minerals from earth to benefit human activity. Povinelli (2016) goes on to argue that maintaining this distinction is one such tactic of late liberalism that is used to benefit those in power, and has become a powerful form of governance. However, as knowledge of human-induced climate change has strengthened, this has challenged any clear sense of a distinction between humans and other phenomena that might be regarded as "non-living" such as climate conditions or earthly formations. So much so that we (humans) must now "watch on" as climate change has come back to "govern" us (Povinelli, 2016). We can no longer ignore the challenges and must sit up and take notice. In this context, it is arguable that climate change is triggering the collapse of the division between life and non-life that, according to Povinelli's notion of geontopower, has been the foundation of governance and power for so long.

For Povinelli (2016), the problematic here is *not* that the division between life and non-life is breaking down, but that we ever conceived such a division in the first place. The division has never made sense, but rather has provided a convenient tactic and framework for those in power to justify destructive or oppressive activity. Povinelli draws on her work and friendship with Indigenous peoples in Australia who have known for millennia that to talk of existence means much more than to say things live or die, or that beings or things are living or non-living. With her colleagues, Povinelli (2016) engages with different modes of existence through formations such as rocks and minerals, bones, creeks, sea reefs and fog. Povinelli is not so interested in whether we can look at the life/non-life distinction from the perspective of what might be perceived as non-life phenomenon, but rather she invites us to consider how we can refuse the division itself (Povinelli, 2020).

Given that fog formations have featured numerous times in our own weather work, we take up Povinelli's invitation to rethink fog as a form of existence via its relations and impact on other existents. Povinelli tells of the *tjelbak*, or morning fog, that is thick and heavy one day when she is out on camp with her Aboriginal aunts and mothers. The *tjelbak*, she is told, is alive and will smell whether she was "proper" to that country. In relation to the *tjelbak* and other such existents, "a person needed, therefore, to watch and smell and listen to how one was being watched and smelled and heard" (Povinelli, 2016, p. 94). Povinelli is not suggesting that the fog has agency in the same way we might attribute to humans, but rather that there are ways in which fog governs us and fog formations can change through our actions. We breathe in fog and it breathes in us (Povinelli, 2020). Reminiscent of our earlier discussion on weather bodies, there is no inside or outside. Rather than see the fog as inert and requiring no responsibility, Povinelli suggests we ask: how might we attend to things that exist? And – in ethical terms – what responsibility could we take for keeping some formations in existence and not overrunning others? For example, when fog becomes smog, it can choke off forms of existence and can carry the truth of the consequences of human activity such as pollution. Conceptualising existents like fog or smog as somehow having boundaries when they are both inside and

122 Relations: Weathering with more-than-human worlds

outside, is problematic and artificial. Instead, Povinelli (2020) asks us to consider how we can appreciate and attend to these as all manifestations of existence.

In the following reflection, Tonya walks and thinks with fog in an attempt to undo assumptions about the inertness and non-liveliness of fog.

> *In the fog, we can lose our sense of direction, but what might we find if we attune with our senses to the touch, smell and taste of fog? In the part of the country where we conduct our research, fog appears in the morning. It hangs low — and in a similar formation to the tjelbak — it snakes and hovers along rivers. Walking through fog, it seems to clear in the spaces around bodies as they move. I breathe in fog and sense the moisture in the air. I begin to ask, "where do I end and where does the fog begin?" But, remembering Povinelli, I realise this question doesn't make sense. The question comes from an imaginary that insists I see myself as a live being separate from an inert fog. Yet, there is no inside or outside. Also, I realise, my imagination has only got so far as to imagine the fog in relation to my movement and my body. What if — as with the tjelbak — I could come to understand fog as a form of existence that could smell or sense me? Would fog sense I belong or not to this land? How might I recognise fog differently and what responsibility do I have to the formation of smog?*
>
> *(Rooney, 2021b)*

Just as fog snakes along the river, and smells us out, so too has climate change come to find us and is demanding our attention. In response, our approach to environmental education attempts to shake off the imaginary that seeks to separate out living and non-living, and instead attends to things through a sense of mutual existence and possibility for endurance. (Povinelli, 2020) Understanding a weather phenomenon such as fog as a lively existent that demands our closer attention, is one such starting point for a more relational approach to learning with weather.

It the context of Povinelli's discussion, it is interesting to note the following insights from the Bawaka collective on people, computers, data and the elements (both chemical and meteorological) when they say that climate change

> *does not live in statistics on paper or models on a computer as if the paper/computer was an artefact that could have an existence separate from humans, from the trees and metals that grew it, from the humidity or the mites or from the ways these things all come into being together.*
>
> *(Bawaka Country et al., 2020, p. 301)*

This reiterates the notion that to continue framing things via a distinction between living and non-living can act as a barrier to how we think about climate change, and how in the context of how things come into being and continue on in other forms, it is a distinction that is hard to sustain. Minerals and geologies from distant times and places find their way into our liveliness and existence, and yet it is the contemporary experience of human-induced climate change that

Earth and deep weather times **123**

leads us to a much older and deeper wisdom of what has always been an ongoing entanglement of people, earth, weather and climate.

Although human-induced climate change might force us to wake up and take notice of the challenges we face, this does not make solutions easy. And Povinelli (2016) suggests "the type of change necessary … will have to be so significant that what we are will no longer be" (p. 40). Once again, we see a call for change that requires a whole rethinking of human relations with climates and worlds. By calling into question the division between living and non-living, Povinelli has led us to reflect on a foundational construct that has underpinned much of how we have been taught about the world in traditional Western education systems.

In concluding, we now turn to the significance of this thinking for environmental education and consider what pedagogical approaches to the temporalities of earth, weather and climate might inform responsive and recuperative climate change practices.

Conclusion

There is a body of recent scholarship on the value of thinking with diverse times and places in reframing environmental education in the context of climate change. (see for example, Duhn, 2012; Duhn, 2017; Hackett & Sommerville, 2017; Pacini-Ketchabaw & Kummen, 2016; Poelina et al., 2022; Rooney, 2019; Somerville, 2013). This new work helps us to think differently about how a more diverse view of temporality might inform perspectives we bring to our work with young children. As the discussion above suggests, there is value in shifting away from an approach to environmental education that is primarily oriented towards the future, to something more situated in the happenings of the "here-ish" and "nowish" (Povinelli, 2016). Learning that is designed to proceed in a linear fashion towards a future goal, might lead us to overlook the significance of actions and ongoingness of our current work practices and decisions. It might also create separation between the happenings of pasts, presents and futures, when these are all deeply interconnected. If we focus learning on the possibilities in noticing how things are happening and moving together, we can still work with and for the urgencies that require us to live and think differently, but we can do so without neglecting the connections between what might seem an ordinary, situated encounter and deeper climates, times and worlds. Learning with weather can help to draw attention to the overlapping times of diverse life worlds and invite us to attend to the many times and places that converge in the "thick present" in which we are living, teaching and learning. The relations that are in, and exceed, this time and place are rich with possibilities from which to develop responsiveness to climate challenges. As we have noted in other writings:

> We notice that while the children may often be focused on the immediate happenings in the present, this does not mean they lack awareness of wider timescales or the lived times of other creatures. … On our walks,

seemingly ordinary moments are richly stacked with multiple pasts and yet-to-be becomings; moments that the children wonder at as they follow leads to imagine other possible worlds and times.

(Rooney, 2019)

Thinking with the times, relations and geological forces that converge in everyday moments, are thus a significant part of children's relations with more-than-human worlds. Taking the time to notice and attend to the complexities of these relations can help us think differently about what it means to learn with weather worlds of other times and places that are inevitably entangled in our more immediate and sensory weather encounters.

References

Bawaka Country, Wright, S., Suchet-Pearson, S., Lloyd, K., Burarrwanga, L., Ganambarr, R., Ganambarr-Stubbs, M., Ganambarr, B., & Maymuru, D. (2020). Gathering of the clouds: Attending to Indigenous understandings of time and climate through songspirals. *Geoforum, 108,* 295–304. https://doi.org/10.1016/j.geoforum.2019.05.017

Chen, M. Y. (2012). *Animacies: Biopolitics, racial mattering, and queer affect.* Duke University Press.

Duhn, I. (2012) Places for pedagogies, pedagogies for places. *Contemporary Issues in Early Childhood,* 13(2), 99–107. https://doi.org/10.2304/ciec.2012.13.2.99

Duhn, I. (2017). Cosmopolitics of place: Towards urban multispecies living in precarious times. In K. Malone, T. Gray, & S. Truong (Eds.), *Reimagining sustainability in precarious times* (1st ed., pp. 45–57). Springer. https://doi.org/10.1007/978-981-10-2550-1_4

Eliasson, O. (2003). Museums are radical. In O. Eliasson & S. May (Eds.), *The weather project,* (pp. 129–138). Tate Publishing.

Hackett, A., & Sommerville, M. (2017). Posthuman literacies: Young children moving in time, place and more-than-human worlds. *Journal of Early Childhood Literacy,* 17(3). 374–391. https://doi.org/10.1177/1468798417704031

Haraway, D. (2016). *Staying with the trouble: Making kin in the Chthulucene.* Duke University Press.

Massey, D. (2005). *For space.* SAGE publishing.

Massey, D. (2006). Landscape as provocation: Reflections on moving mountains. *Journal of Material Culture,* 11(1–2), 33–48.

Merewether, J. (2020) Enchanted animism: A matter of care. *Contemporary Issues in Early Childhood.* https://doi.org/10.1177/1463949120971380

Metcalf, J., & van Dooren, T. (2012). Editorial preface. *Environmental Philosophy,* 9(1), v–xiv.

Mitman, G. (2019). *Reflections on the plantationocene: A conversation with Donna Haraway and Anna Tsing* [Audio Podcast]. Edge Effects. https://edgeeffects.net/haraway-tsing-plantationocene/

Neimanis, A., & Walker, R. L. (2014). Weathering: Climate change and the "thick time" of transcorporeality. *Hypatia,* 29(3), 558–575.

Pacini-Ketchabaw, V., & Kummen, K. (2016). Shifting temporal frames in children's common worlds in the Anthropocene. *Contemporary Issues in Early Childhood,* 17(4), 431–441. https://doi.org/10.1177/1463949116677930

Peters, K. (2021). Writing (extra)planetary geographies of weather-worlds. In K. Barry, M. Borovnik, T. Edensor (Eds.), *Weather: Spaces, mobilities and affects,* (pp. 250–262). Routledge.

Poelina, A., Wooltorton, S., Blaise, M., Aniere, C., Horwitz, P., White, P., & Muecke, S. (2022). Regeneration time: Ancient wisdom for planetary wellbeing. *Australian Journal of Environmental Education*, 1–18. https://doi.org/10.1017/aee.2021.34

Povinelli, E. (2016). *Geontologies: A Requiem to late liberalism.* Duke University Press.

Povinelli, E. (2020, July 8). *When rocks speak* [Audio podcast]. Countersign https://countersignisapodcast.com/podcasts/

Rooney, T. (2019). Weathering time: Walking with young children in a changing climate. *Children's Geographies*, *17*(2), 177–189. https://doi.org/10.1080/14733285.2018.1474172

Rooney, T. (2021a). Moved by wind and storms – Imaginings in a changing landscape. In K. Barry, M. Borovnik, T. Edensor (Eds.), *Weather: Spaces, mobilities and affects*, (pp. 38–50). Routledge.

Rooney, T., (2021b, October 19) Response to 'When Rocks Speak' by Elizabeth Povinelli. *Responsive Roundtable Series: Ecologies in-the-making #6*

Rooney, T., & Royds, F. (2018, August 13) A dry and dusty winter walk. *Weathering Collaboratory: Exploring climate change pedagogies with children.* https://weathercollaboratory.blog/2018/08/13/a-dry-and-dusty-winter-walk/

Somerville, M. (2013). *Water in a dry land: Place-learning through art and story.* Routledge.

Steffen, W., Rockström, J., Richardson, K., Lenton, T., Folke, C., Liverman, C. P., Ummerhayes, A. D., Barnosky, C. S., Crucifix, M., Donges, J., Fetzer, I., Lade, S., Scheffer, M., Winkelmann, R., & Schellnhuber, H. J. (2018) Trajectories of the earth system in the Anthropocene in *Proceedings of the National Academy of Sciences*, *115*(33), 8252–8259. https://doi.org/10.1073/pnas.1810141115

Taylor, A., & Pacini-Ketchabaw, V. (2015) Learning with children, ants, and worms in the Anthropocene: Towards a common world pedagogy of multispecies vulnerability. *Pedagogy, Culture & Society*, *23*(4), 507–529. https://doi.org/10.1080/14681366.2015.1039050

Yusoff, K. (2013). Geologic life: Prehistory, climate, futures in the Anthropocene. *Environment and Planning D: Society and Space*, *31*(5), 779–795.

Yusoff, K. (2015). Geologic subjects: Nonhuman origins, geomorphic aesthetics and the art of becoming inhuman. *Cultural Geographies*, *22*(3), 383–407.

PART IV

Responses: Learning and speculating in a climate change era

9
WEATHER LEARNING

At the start of our walk, a child produces a hand drawn map. This will show us "where to go" she declares. Along the way we find human-made maps and signposts that children study for clues. There are signs in the landscape too. One child looks at the surrounding low hills, valleys and a stand of trees to one side, then points – 'I think it's that way'. The group doesn't get far before a child stops: 'I found a teepee made of sticks.' Soon children are peering into rabbit burrows, pointing out rabbit poo, scratching in orange dirt and following other things that catch their attention. During all this, a reminder from one child: "We need to keep going. We are already here." (pointing to the map)

(Taylor & Rooney, 2017a)

And so goes our walk; a combination of way-finding with maps (see Figure 9.1), landmarks and other clues, dotted by invitations along the way to pause and look more closely at what was happening in the various formations and lives of animals, earth, trees and materials.

The children responded, with alternating attention to what was happening underfoot and in the lives of other critters who also inhabit these common spaces. Why and where they lingered and for how long was, as always, in some way linked to seasonality and weather, for example, through the plants that were in flower, the dryness of soil or the presence of animals and insects. The rhythm, pace and direction of our walking came variously from children, hills and valleys, weathers and creatures. Our path was far from straight-forward.

In this chapter, we draw on our methods of thinking, walking and writing with weather. We propose that early childhood environmental education can be enriched by cultivating what we refer to as *weather learning*, which includes deliberate strategies and practices for learning with weather. We bring together

DOI: 10.4324/9781003150411-13

130 Responses: Learning and speculating in a climate change era

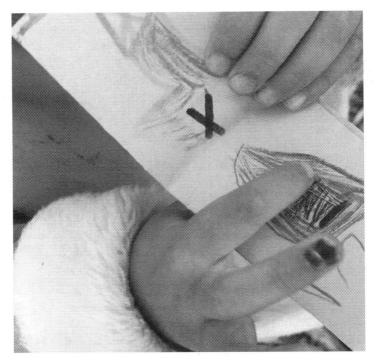

FIGURE 9.1 "We are already here"

ideas of how and why weather learning might be just what we need in a climate change era if early childhood education pedagogy and practice is to be responsive and responsible in shaping weather worlds.

Weather learning aims to do more than draw attention to weather as an important subject in environmental education. It also does more than explain how weather is part of a context in which children learn about the environment and climate. These points are important, but there is so much more to say. We are not promoting weather as a singular unit of inquiry, but rather see weather as something that cannot be understood outside worlds made by and with weather. In our weather walks with children conducted during our research, we would rarely discuss *the weather* in any direct sense. Our interest was rather in the emerging relations and encounters that happened as we walked with weather. Central to this approach is to avoid positioning humans as external onlookers to weather phenomenon and to avoid an emphasis on weather as something we might extract from our surrounds. Rather, it is grounded in an understanding that "we" (humans, plants, animals, rocks, weathers, soils and a multitude of complex ecosystems and planetary matter) are all in this climate situation together. Further, this is not just a scenario for "now" or for deciding what happens next, it is about recognising that there is a convergence (or in Massey's (2005) words a "thrown-togetherness") of weather worlds from deep times and places and matters that meet in the "hereish and nowish" (Povinelli, 2016) and from which weather worlds will continue to emerge, both in spite of and because of human decisions that impact lives in multi-species, mutually vulnerable worlds. The thinking that underpins our approach is not so much new, but is rather a deliberate form of feminist listening, (re)learning, at times (un)learning, (re)thinking and (re)telling stories. Weather learning is dynamic. It is happening when ideas, walking, weather and worlds come together. It is never finished. Instead, it is an ongoing project that acknowledges there will always be uncertainty and unpredictability. It is not a linear step-by-step approach to accumulating knowledge about weather, but rather requires us to circle to other times and happenings such that learning accumulates through bodily weather affects and relations. It is learning that is at times playful, curious and joyful, though never frivolous. Weather learning seeks out connections and stories and ways of living that have been told and held in Earth for many years. It asks, what is happening with weather? What and how do these happenings matter for the shape of weather worlds to come?

In our work with children, we notice they have a particular capacity to attend to what is puzzling, uncertain or unexpected. We see this as they linger in moments and encounters to try and work out what is happening, without necessarily seeking a singular or complete answer. There seems to be no sense that everything needs to be resolved. We also notice that children's everyday encounters open unexpected avenues to explore and test out the limits of vulnerability that comes from living in shared worlds. We have witnessed moments of connection, care and mutual recognition within and between children and more-than-human worlds. When working with young children, we therefore have a unique opportunity to foster and speculate on new ways of thinking with weather that suggest a myriad of exciting pathways to explore in environmental education; ways forward that bring the challenges, concerns and cares of climate change directly into day-to-day classroom practice. This type of environmental learning is thus about much more than building new knowledge of and about the environment, it has an ethical dimension as well. It offers space for us (adults and children) to reflect on what it means for all creatures and ecologies to live well together in shared weather worlds. It is about learning with weather, and recognising that through our work with children, we (adults) may also in turn learn to live better with weather.

Providing times and spaces to nurture this form of weather learning, sits in contrast to traditional approaches to education that focus on solving problems, neat endings and leading children to the *right* answer via adult-directed instruction and scaffolding. We illustrate the points of departure more fully through two examples of weather learning in relation to seasons and weather; first, we examine some early childhood teaching practices on the theme of the seasons in early childhood classrooms, and second, we consider the value and limitations of an inquiry learning approach to weather.

132 Responses: Learning and speculating in a climate change era

Learning about seasons in early childhood education

Early childhood education is replete with creative and rich approaches to learning about the weather, ranging from song, dance and story to art and science explorations. These can nurture children's imagination and promote collective and intergenerational learning such as through sharing of childhood songs. There are, however, some teaching strategies and resources used in early childhood classrooms that provide a more limited opportunity to learn about and with weather. As we have written about elsewhere (Rooney et al., 2021), it is common in early childhood for the teaching day to start with a group activity around a weather wheel, calendar or chart. While this can establish routine and build an understanding of changes in weather, we found that there were also tensions "because the activities and resources used tend to be based on simplified and separable weather concepts that are presented as widespread or universal, sometimes bearing little resemblance to local conditions" (Rooney et al., 2021, p. 115). So, for example, a chart might use symbols for sun, clouds or wind (a bit like a weather report) but leave little room for discussion about the shifts that might happen across a day. This activity can provide children with some mode of connection to the outside weather world, where for example this is linked to discussions around suitable clothing, hats or footwear, and in this sense offers a starting point for building connections between children and weather.

There are other activities that do not work as well in providing connection to the context in which children learn. In the following instructions for a simple activity about the seasons, teachers are advised:

> To teach the seasons, use pictures and books to describe each seasonal change such as piles of dry leaves for autumn, snow for winter, the beach for summer and flowers for spring.
>
> *(Care for Kids, 2020)*

This activity promotes features of seasons that bear little resemblance to seasonal changes or conditions in many places across Australia. As the Bureau of Meteorology (2015) explains:

> Australia's climate is diverse. Monsoon tropics, desert, savannah, alpine and temperate regions can all be found in various locations. The sheer diversity of ecological zones can't be meaningfully simplified to a rigid European seasonal calendar for the entire continent.
>
> *(para. 30)*

The activity described above is therefore more of an artificial construct that draws together *ideas* of what seasons *might* look like and is disconnected from any specific locality given that concepts snow and beach would rarely be found together. This over-simplification limits the pedagogical potential of the activity in several ways. It prioritises a generalised notion of seasons at the expense of anything genuine or local that children might experience or connect with in the places where they are learning. It is also an example of an imposed (in this case Northern hemisphere) construct or framework on an area of learning, and in doing so privileges this knowledge system over local knowledge. As we have noted elsewhere,

> [w]here there is a disconnect between a learning activity and local weather conditions, there is also a risk this might perpetuate an understanding of weather as somehow distant, abstract and removed from situated knowledges and relations.
>
> (Rooney et al., 2021, p. 115)

It should be noted that there are examples of season-based approaches to environmental learning that in Northern hemisphere contexts could foster meaningful connection in some localities (for example, see Watts, 2013). This is a reminder of the importance of providing context and connection in environmental learning activities.

Later in this chapter, we turn to the significance of learning that offers a stronger sense of connection and recognition of local seasonal change and the rhythms of weather, and how we might attend to this in young children's education. Before doing so, we turn to a second example of a common approach to education on the theme of weather.

Learning about weather through inquiry

Inquiry learning is a valuable approach in environmental education insofar as it tends to draw on children's curiosity, strives for engagement, can involve outdoor activities and sensory learning, and teaches strategies for science learning that children can build on in later years. One important aspect of the inquiry resource described below is that it encourages a localised examination of weather, offering children a meaningful mode of connection to the worlds around them. There remain, however, some limitations in this form of learning when applied to environmental education in the context of wider climate change challenges.

Much of the teaching about weather and seasons in the early years of school in Australia adopts a Western approach to science teaching. There is acknowledgement of other types of weather knowledge, such as insights from Indigenous cultures, but it is Western science that acts as the dominant evidence base for what constitutes knowledge. The Primary Connections unit of work and teaching resource titled *Weather in my world* is designed for foundation year students (around age 5 years). It adopts an inquiry-based approach to learning and encourages children to seek out knowledge in different ways, including through observation, the senses and measuring different weather phenomena such as wind and rain. The emphasis is on bringing together various threads to reflect on "what we have learned about weather" (Australian Academy of Science, 2020, p. 32). The

134 Responses: Learning and speculating in a climate change era

purpose behind such learning is also often explicitly linked to locality, interconnections and sustainability:

> *Students investigate the relationship between components of the weather system—the air, Sun and wind—and develop an appreciation for the interconnectedness of these components. This can assist them to develop the knowledge, skills and values necessary for people to act in ways that contribute to more sustainable patterns of living.*
> *(Australian Academy of Science, 2020, p. xv)*

In acknowledging that there may be other ways of thinking beyond the "Western science way of making evidence-based claims about daily and seasonal changes" (Australian Academy of Science, 2020, p. xv), the *Weather in my world* teaching resource notes that:

> *Through thousands of years of observation, Indigenous culture has developed a deep understanding of environmental indicators to predict weather patterns. Some Indigenous people use their own seasonal calendars based on knowledge of the sequence of events in their local environment.*
> *(Australian Academy of Science, 2020, p. 4)*

While these descriptions highlight some of the valuable features of inquiry learning mentioned earlier, there are also limitations for how children might come to understand their connections with and within weather worlds. The first is that emphasis remains focused on learning "about" weather in a way that situates weather as separate and observable. This reinforces the notion of weather as something discrete from human and other life; thus providing few openings for children to consider the mutuality of weathering, weather world making and intricacies of human–weather relations. Secondly, weather is presented as a phenomenon that, if we observe it correctly, will tell us (humans) something about the day or the season or (over time) changes in the climate. It is something we can learn from for our own human benefit or survival. This human-centric lens doesn't acknowledge or account for the lively presence of other weather companions. Finally, the way in which Indigenous knowledge is presented as an alternative in this resource sets up a hierarchy of weather knowledge where what is Western is considered both *science* and evidence-based, while non-Western (in this case Indigenous knowledges) is positioned as *not science* and the learning from stories, songs and the land itself as not really *evidence*. An inquiry learning approach with these features thus only takes us so far and doesn't seem to extend to an exploration of the significance of embeddedness, relationality, active materiality, diverse temporalities and mutual world making as part of learning with weather worlds.

This example of the *Weather in my world* resource is only one of many in a range of resources that teachers might use to teach children about weather and the environment. We selected this as an example as it does offer many of the opportunities and potential we have talked about in this book; making the most of children's curiosity, learning outdoors, a questioning approach and multi-sensory engagement with weather, to name a few. Yet, even with these similarities, there is still much more that can be done to promote a richer form of weather learning; one that positions children (and humans) as part of the weather worlds they notice, listen to, reach out to and connect with in ways that are open-ended and uncertain. Our suggestion is that environmental education will need to make room for these possibilities, if children are to engage more deeply with weather, climate and changing worlds. To expand on this, we now look more closely at how we might learn with the rhythms of weather and seasonality in ways that are locally relevant and at the same time offer a point of connection to wider climate change.

Rhythms of weather

In this section, we ask what would happen if we looked to place and weather for clues of seasonal change, rather than relying on calendars and constructs that have little alignment with what happens in various places across Australia? Once again, we focus on Australia because it is where we conducted our research; hopefully, these ideas can be expanded and adapted to other regions.

During our research, we would at times find ourselves or the children describing seasonality in terms of Summer, Autumn, Winter and Spring. For example, noticing the Acacia blossoms on one walk, a child commented "It's like spring" (Taylor & Rooney, 2017b), and we noted in one of our blog posts that it was "our first wintery walk" (Rooney & Royds, 2018) for the year. It was interesting how easily we fell to this seasonal language to describe changes in temperature, plants and other phenomena in the landscape. In early summer, we would also talk to the young children about keeping safe around snakes. Children knew to keep out of the tall grass in the warmer months so as not to startle a snake. Signs also appeared during snake season.

For the most part, we didn't directly think, walk or write using the framing of the four seasons. Our interest was more in looking for clues in the landscape, waterways or skies for what might be happening in the lives of other critters and plants. As we did so, we wondered if there was a different way of thinking about the shifts, flows and rhythms of weather that attended more to what was happening, rather than only seeing this through a lens of seasonal change that has been adopted from another continent and hemisphere.

The writing of Deborah Bird Rose has helped us think through the tensions and uneasiness that we experienced when thinking about weather through a Eurocentric seasonal calendar. Rose (2005) explains that there are alternative ways to think about seasonality in Australia that are localised and that articulate the interconnectedness of elements and ecologies. Indigenous weather knowledges are rich with detail on seasonal change that is localised and that moves with the rhythms and interconnectedness of elements, plants, animals, seas and land. It is a way of thinking with seasons that is dynamic rather than static, that permits variation and unpredictability, and yet also makes sense of concurrent happenings

136 Responses: Learning and speculating in a climate change era

(Rose, 2005). For example, from one of a series of calendars developed by traditional owners in collaboration with the CSIRO (2021) to capture some of the local Indigenous seasonal ecological knowledge, we learn that in the Larrakia seasonal year (on land also known as Darwin) there are seven seasons; *Balnba* (rainy season), *Dalay* (monsoon season), *Mayilema* (speargrass, Magpie Goose egg and knock 'em down season), *Damibila* (barramundi and bush fruit time), *Dinidjanggama* (heavy dew time), *Gurrulwa guligi* (big wind time) and *Dalirrgang* (build-up). This seasonal knowledge is rich with signs, relations, connections and practices; for example, between *Gurrulwa guligi* and *Dalirrgang,* we learn that:

> *Freshwater mangrove fruit signify it is time to hunt Gakkingga (Magpie Goose). It is a time of feasting on the flood plains. Ngamamba (Cycad nuts) are ready for harvest. Banimadla (Long-necked Turtle) spend time under the ground waiting for the rains. The Cocky Apple (possum tucker) drops a carpet of white flowers. Their sweet scent signals that the build-up has arrived.*
>
> *(Williams et al., 2012)*

This expression of seasonality captures some of the many happenings in weather worlds. These are things that happen concurrently and as a result of a multitude of factors and conditions coming together. Unexpected events may lead to unpredictable happenings, but this is part of – not erased from – this system of seasonal knowledge (Rose, 2005).

We can see this as an example of weather knowledge that captures the rhythms and flows and interconnections of climatic and season change, and yet does not resort to superficial erasure of *tidying up* of unexpected weather events. We can also see why, as Rose (2005) suggests, any attempts to "fit" an understanding of Indigenous seasons within the Western constructs of seasonality will risk silencing or simplifying Indigenous knowledges of weather and ecologies that have been developed over many thousands of years. It seems likely however that these knowledges have much to offer how we might learn and live with climate change over time, and it is therefore important to make space for diverse weather knowledges and ways of knowing weather.

In thinking about weather and seasonality, there is much more happening that can be captured by a regular, rigid and (Western) universally applied framework of what the seasons might look like. The weather learning practices described in this book invoke learning with land, wind, change and happenings that are localised and yet also considers ways children might make connections between seemingly minor or ordinary weather learning events and wider climatic change. It also involves making room for what is unpredictable, unexpected and perhaps surprising, and looking to these for clues and signs, even when we do not have answers for children as to what these signs might mean. Rose (2005) suggests that "the rhythms of things that happen simultaneously are crucial codes for knowing what is happening in the world. Some of this knowledge is dispersed widely, but most is highly localised" (p. 40). We understand this as drawing attention to the over-lapping lives, times and happenings of multiple weather worlds that cannot be separated or represented as singular, linear or predictable. This multiplicity acknowledges diverse times of more-than-human creatures and materials, as discussed in previous chapters. Anna Tsing (2019) also provides a useful notion to think with here; the idea of *polyphonic assemblages*. Drawing on the musical form of polyphonic music, where "autonomous melodies intertwine," Tsing (2019) describes a particular form of noticing where the listener is forced to pick out "separate, simultaneous melodies and to listen for the moments of harmony and dissonance they created together" (p. 232). This practice, Tsing suggests can help us to appreciate "multiple temporal rhythms and trajectories" (p. 232). This idea of polyphony, and the practice of attuning one's ear to multiple entwined melodies, reminds us of how we might listen with weather as it flows with and through bodies, histories, cultures, places and climates. There are many stories to tell with weather, and the practice weather learning invites us to try attuning to multiple interwoven weather happenings, to emerging relations and convergences, to unexpected riffs and to a seasonality that is locally interdependent with land, rocks and multi-species others, including humans.

Weather learning – A pedagogical shift

We have covered much weather ground in this book. In this section, we briefly re-cap some key messages as they relate to pedagogy and practice and explain the pedagogical shift that is required if we are to collectively work together towards a mode of learning that is more responsive and connected to the climate challenges of our time. First, a reminder that for us, this project has not been about learning something new, but rather a process of letting go of our preconceived ideas of what it means to teach young children and to rethink the basis of our relationship with the (weather) content and material we wanted to teach. We have said earlier that this work is not easy and it is imperfect. We still find ourselves (in conversation, in writing and in practice) reverting to child-centric frameworks and having to once again (re)orient our positioning to one of learning *with* weather; this is very much an ongoing process of collective learning. The material we have presented in this book reflects different points on our own learning journey, and in this sense remains open to further thinking and doing.

We opened this book by saying that the crisis of climate change offers both a challenge and opportunity for educators – and above all, a chance to think more deeply about human relations with worlds. To achieve significant change, however, we need an approach to learning that:

- redirects the focus from human-centred positioning;
- resists certainty and containment to embrace what is uncertain, unbounded and unruly;
- makes room to consider the ethical dimensions of living in climate worlds; and
- allows us to reimagine different weather worlds.

138 Responses: Learning and speculating in a climate change era

This work is not just about thinking and reflecting, it is also about doing, walking, writing, moving and making worlds together with weather and our more-than-human companions in ways that allow all to flourish. Further, this can only be achieved in education if we look beyond the traditional frameworks of child development and learning to the potential of postdevelopmentalism. It is from this positioning that we can imagine, speculate and generate new knowledges and worlds, while also acknowledging the historical and colonial underpinnings that for too long have silenced other voices and ways of knowing weather and worlds.

The key message and contribution that we want this work to make is for the field of early childhood education to consider weather learning as feminist practice. We are interested in weather learning that is place-situated, embodied, relational and ethical. Our bodily, sensory and affective engagement with weather brings us closer to understanding ourselves in relation to and *as* weather, and provides a conduit for stronger relations with wider climate worlds. In early childhood education, and the whole field of environmental education, there needs to be more room for this kind of open and speculative learning. Without this, we may not get close enough to understanding, connecting and responding to the climate challenges of our times. And we may fail to nurture deep weather knowledges that children might carry with them as they continue to forge and build worlds together with others who also share and rely on liveable weather worlds.

Through our research, we discovered a multitude of pedagogical opportunities of thinking, walking and writing with weather; some challenged our preconceived ideas about teaching and learning; some required us to listen and learn differently; and others invited us to look at the small and seemingly insignificant events and relations to notice things we may have otherwise overlooked. Learning with weather is a kind of lingering and listening to and with weather worlds. What might we hear if we become more attuned to stories of wind, rain and sunshine? Is it possible that we might come to see ourselves differently as weather bodies and agents of change in weather worlds to come?

Weather learning takes time: time for children to attend to encounters and for relations with place and other species to emerge, build and evolve into ways of knowing worlds; and time for us as teachers and researchers to notice children's learning differently through weather. We do not have to be direct or didactic about the presence of weather in our teaching so that it becomes separated out, but rather seek out ways to notice and express weather learning that is entangled, seasonal, local, elemental, both routine and unexpected, and affective.

Making rain

We share here one final weather story that perhaps most fully brought our attention to understanding children as collective weather makers with lake, trees, sunshine and wind (see Figure 9.2).

Weather learning   **139**

FIGURE 9.2 Making rain

The soft dying fronds on the fallen branches of Casuarina trees are turning brown. Children each spend time finding the perfect branch. They dip these into the water, then lift them to witness gentle drips. Soon children are watering plants, land, us and each other.

> "It's a rain cloud."
> "Everyone grab a stick."
> "It's raining, raining, raining."
> "It's a rainy day today."

One child holds their dripping stick over a nearby patch of grass:

> "I'm making some of these grow."
> "You get the water on the stick and then shake it, shake it off."
> "Watch out. Here comes the real rain."
> "I'm going to make some more rain."
> "It's raining, it's pouring. We love the rain."

Someone begins singing:

> "It's a rain branch. It's raining, raining. It's a rainy day today."
> "I'm going to make some of these [plants] grow."
> "You shake it, shake it, and it rains."
> "Hey, I found an old drink bottle. That's rubbish."

140 Responses: Learning and speculating in a climate change era

> *"I found a ball. I found this. That's a cigarette lighter. You light with it."*
> *"People just throw rubbish in the water everywhere."*
> *"I can see seagulls. Seagulls are coming."*
> *"I'm going to make more rain. Watch out! Here comes the real rain. It's raining, it's pouring. We love the rain."*
>
> *(Rooney & Royds, 2018)*

We found out after this walk that the children had been learning about drought in the classroom and were raising funds to support the farmers. We were uncertain what prompted the children to start this rain-making activity with fallen branches. Was it the classroom discussion that somehow awoke a desire to make some much needed rain? Was it our previous walks across a dusty landscape, that also made children somehow aware of the need for rain? Or did the presence of the soft branches near the water's edge, and the sunshine making its way through the branches, act as an invitation to reach out to the cool water and shower each other with glistening drops? Either way, the children seemed captivated by this curious form of weather making as they shaped their own rain patterns. This is weather learning; a feminist mode of learning with and from weather, of being weather and shaping weather worlds where all might flourish. It is learning that did not come from adults nor only from the children, but rather from the convergence of branches, water, sunlight, drought, walking, singing and children's playful imagination. This was weather worlds in the making.

This story shows a kind of responsiveness to weather and wider climatic patterns that is different from what we might witness in a traditional classroom activity about the weather. It reveals acts of care and of moving with, shaping and responding to rhythms of weather. Yet, at the same time it is not a form of education that comes from a starting point where children are told they must care for the environment, which can sometimes revert to a *human as saviour* positioning that risks perpetuating the view that children are somehow separate from and superior to the world they are acting upon (Nxumalo, 2018; Taylor, 2017) Weather learning fosters responsiveness that is neither singular in focus nor disconnected from specific places and times. We think of it as an opportunity that makes possible "myriad place-based and pluralist responses that nourish different kinds of worldings" (Wright et al., 2020, p. 295).

Conclusion: Rethinking environmental education

We have barely touched the surface of the pedagogical potential of learning with weather. Weather is often discomforting and messy. Human responses seem to shift wildly from a desire to control, contain and master wild weather on the one hand, to on the other simply throwing up our hands and saying it is all out of our control and there is nothing we can do. However, the implausibility of continually framing such understandings in ways that posit *weather* and *humans* as separate, requires us to move beyond this type of thinking to recognise that we (humans) are weather.

The opportunity to learn with complex weather worlds offers more than simply a point of sensory connection with weather; though this in itself remains critical as a knowledge-rich affective encounter with other weather bodies. Attending to weather both in and around us – including the bodily affects of weather and multi-species weather relations – offers a mode of connection wider climatic activity. It helps us to recognise our (human) interconnectedness to the wildness of weather worlds. We thus understand environmental education as a lively practice of thinking, doing and writing *with* weather so as to foster growing awareness of our own (human) part in the shaping and making of weather worlds. Walking with children helps to ground our practices in places that matter and brings us into proximity with the lives, times, and worlds of multi-species companions. And it provides children with the opportunity to notice, to reach out, to imagine, to speculate and to experiment with what it means to weather worlds together with others.

References

Australian Academy of Science. (2020). *Weather in my world.* https://primaryconnections. org.au/resources-and-pedagogies/curriculum-units/weather-my-world

Bureau of Meteorology. (2015). *Introduction to climate culture – A history of Aboriginal and Torres Strait Islander culture.* http://www.bom.gov.au/iwk/culture.shtml

Care for Kids. (2020, October 21). *Learning about seasons with autumn colours.* https://www. careforkids.com.au/child-care-provider-articles/article/565/learning-about-seasons-with-autumn-colours

CSIRO. (2021). *About the Indigenous seasons calendars.* https://www.csiro.au/en/research/ natural-environment/land/about-the-calendars

Massey, D. (2005) *For space.* SAGE Publishing.

Nxumalo, F. (2018) Stories for living on a damaged planet: Environmental education in a preschool classroom. *Journal of Early Childhood Research*, 16(2), 148–159. https://doi. org/10.1177/1476718X17715499

Povinelli, E. (2016). *Geontologies: A Requiem to late liberalism.* Duke University Press.

Rooney, T., Blaise, M., & Royds, F. (2021). With shadows, dust and mud: Activating weathering-with pedagogies in early childhood education. *Contemporary Issues in Early Childhood*, 22(2), 109–123. https://doi.org/10.1177%2F1463949120939202

Rooney, T., & Royds, F. (2018) Making rain. *Weathering Collaboratory: Exploring climate change pedagogies with children.* https://weathercollaboratory.blog/2018/10/03/making-rain/

Rose, D. (2005). Rhythms, patterns, connectivities: Indigenous concepts of seasons and change. In T. Sherratt, T. Griffiths, & L. Robin (Eds.), *A change in the weather: Climate and culture in Australia*, (pp. 32–41). National Museum of Australia.

Taylor, A., (2017) Beyond stewardship: Common world pedagogies for the Anthropocene. *Environmental Education Research*, 23(10), 1448–1461. https://doi.org/10.1080/13504622. 2017.1325452

Taylor, A., & Rooney, T. (2017a, July 19). Finding our way – Maps and signs. *Walking with Wildlife in Wild Weather Times – A Common World Childhoods Research Collective Blog.* https://walkingwildlifewildweather.com/2017/07/19/finding-our-way-maps-and-signs/

Taylor, A., & Rooney, T. (2017b, August 16). Shifts and flows. *Walking with Wildlife in Wild Weather Times-A Common World Childhoods Research Collective Blog.* https://walking wildlifewildweather.com/2017/08/16/shifts-and-flows/

Tsing, A. L., (2019) When the things we study respond to each other: Tools for unpacking "the material". In P. Harvey, C. Krohn-Hansen, & K.G., Nustad (Eds.), *Anthropos and the material*, (pp. 221–243). Duke University Press, (see https://www.dukeupress.edu/anthropos-and-the-material).

Watts, A., (2013) *Outdoor learning through the seasons: An essential guide for the early years*. Routledge.

Williams, L., Williams, J., Oogden, M., Risk, K., Risk, A., & Woodward, E. (2012). *Gulumoerrgin Seasons (calendar): Larrakia, Darwin, Northern Territory, Australia*. CSIRO (Land and Water).

Wright, S., Suchet-Pearson, K., Lloyd, L., Burarrwanga, R., Ganambarr, M., Ganambarr-Stubbs, B., Ganambarr, D., & Maymuru, D. (2020). Gathering of the clouds: Attending to indigenous understandings of time and climate through songspirals. *Geoforum, 108*(2020), 295–304. https://doi.org/10.1016/j.geoforum.2019.05.017

10
CONCLUSION

An invitation to weather together

The exploration of weather relations with bodies, multi-species worlds, and times and places in the third part of this book shows that weather is more than a backdrop to our day-to-day lives or simply a feature of what is happening outside. Weather is life, death and decay and the interconnected ongoingness of worlds. Weather is a maker of worlds and times, and in many ways we too are weather. What we do with weather therefore matters. We are not just in weather worlds, we are part of weather worlds. The changing climate that we witness in the *hereish* and *nowish* is not disconnected, but happening through bodies, lives, places, atmospheres, biologies and geologies of Earth and space. Wild weather brings wind and storms to homes and habitats, it brings extremes of rain and sunshine to food production, and creates unexpected rifts in the ongoing rhythms and cycles of ecosystems. Weather can help us thrive, but it is also what makes us vulnerable. Weather reveals the mutual vulnerability of all existents who share common worlds.

Why does this matter in environmental education? It matters because it impacts on the approach and perspective we bring to teaching and learning. To adopt the view that we (humans) can be *masters* of change both ignores our mutual vulnerability within weather worlds and overlooks the ways that action and change centred on human concerns will exacerbate the problems we already face. This is not to say that we cannot generate meaningful changes in our pedagogy and practice – we can and we do so all the time. However, what is important is that in the context of climate change, we can no longer continue to teach by positioning ourselves *outside or separate from* the doing and making of worlds. We need to recognise that we are living and teaching *with* worlds, and it is only from this positioning that we can come to understand the significance of ordinary, embodied encounters as points of connection that matter, and as a positioning from which we might change and generate better worlds together.

DOI: 10.4324/9781003150411-14

144 Responses: Learning and speculating in a climate change era

Understanding worlds as also weather worlds, helps to draw attention to the proximity of our bodies, lives and relations to climate change (Neimanis & Walker, 2014). Paying attention to what is minor or ordinary is part of our feminist practice, as it involves questioning that which is positioned as dominant or important and makes space for other ways of knowing and being-with that are often silenced and ignored. Attending to the ordinary and learning to be affected by worlds we are part of is an "adventure of worlding" (Haraway, 2013, p. 9); of imagining and speculating together the possibilities of weather worlds to come where we recognise what is at stake for all lives, ecologies, times and places. Thus, we have an ethical responsibility not just to take climate change seriously, but to better understand and respond to the implications that exceed our human presence and needs.

As humans grappling with our own place in the world, ethical and political dimensions arise from human entanglements in climate changes and futures. We end our book not with a neat and tidy conclusion, but instead with an invitation for you, the reader, to respond with us by weathering together. Weathering together recognises that that "'we' are in *this* together" and that 'we'-are–not-one-and-the-same-but-we-differ" (Braidotti, 2022, p. 8). Weather learning with animals, plants, sky, seas, and each other is the beginning, but it is nowhere near finished. Because weathering together is an ongoing project, there is so much more thinking and doing to be done. We take up the provocations of feminist scholars Donna Haraway (2016) and Maria Puig de la Bellacasa (2017), as an opening to speculate on what it means to participate in the more-than-human collective and to generate weather world making and *weathering together.*

The figure of SF

We learn how feminist speculation works through Donna Haraway's (2016) figure of SF. Haraway's scholarship is full of figures (cyborg, pigeons, dogs) and they are used both metaphorically and literally to think through and respond to semiotic and material issues often related to subject-object and nature-culture boundaries, binaries and hierarchies. Thinking with these figures is a playfully serious mode of practice. And it is a situated practice that happens from within worlds, not by standing outside of them. This situated practice simply cannot be done alone; it is a collective endeavour.

Instead of naming one figure, SF stands for many things: "science fiction, speculative fabulation, string figures, speculative feminism, science fact, so far." (Haraway, 2016, p. 2). Feminist speculation is an adventurous thinking and making process. It is important to remember that it is not just about imagining in our heads what might be, either in the present or the future. That kind of thought is characteristic of human exceptionalism and is transcendental, because it actively separates out the human from what is happening in the hereish and nowish, and it perpetuates a binary of mind over body. For speculation, imagination is necessary, but it must not stay in our heads. To speculate is to imagine, and speculation is a methodology insisting "on the co-constitutive role of the embedded observer, the perspective and the rich agentiality (multi-subjectivity) of context itself" (Åsberg et al., 2015, p. 151). It is therefore an ethical endeavour because "decisions must take place somehow in the presence of those who will bear those consequences" (Haraway, 2013 p. 22). By understanding speculation as a situated and relational practice of thinking and doing, similar to what Sarah Truman does in her research-creation projects (see Truman, 2021 for an overview), the speculative adventure of *weathering together* becomes an ethical knowledge building project. It is an example of worlding together with weather.

The speculative brings together the factual, the fictional and the fabulated. It is a practice of giving and receiving with more-than-human others; a situated practice, which prevents it becoming a universal or abstract kind of thing. It is hard work because you must constantly keep *at this, not that*. This means that decisions must be made. It also requires a returning. Returning involves so many things; going back to a place over and over again; picking up on ideas or happenings, while always making room for more. As Haraway (2013) says, SF is about "dropping threads and so mostly failing but sometimes finding something that works, something consequential and maybe even beautiful, that wasn't there before" (p. 13). Crafting the conditions for flourishing is what makes this pedagogical. Telling stories with place and weather can also be part of pedagogical practices for creating and sharing connections that matter. Playing and singing with weather can both exceed and bring together thinking and doing; and are thus speculative practices that – whether they illuminate or muddy the complexities of child-weather relations – are about going on together.

Our invitation to speculate with weather together is therefore a "risky proposition" (Haraway, 2013, p. 15) that requires a shift in perspective from *outside* weather, to recognising that we *are* weather. It also requires us to accept that much may remain unknown or feel far too open. The happenings may seem ordinary at times, and we might find ourselves wishing for something that moves a little more quickly or with a stronger sense of singular purpose. We may also feel a sense of vulnerability that cannot be easily smoothed over and may face questions that cannot be easily resolved (or ever). These are some of the tensions of learning with weather that cannot be ignored. Importantly, it is these often disconcerting affects that help us to recognise that weather learning is happening. This type of weather learning matters because it is also a practice of care.

Responsiveness as an invitation to care

Puig de la Bellacasa (2017) encourages us to think with a notion of care in ways that acknowledge the tensions associated with this concept, and like Haraway, suggests that we try to resist the "tendencies to smooth out" any apparent difficulties (p. 11). For Puig de la Bellacasa, the practice of care is non-innocent

146 Responses: Learning and speculating in a climate change era

and rich with tension and mutual obligations, and this recognition lies at the heart of living together. As discussed earlier in this book, Puig de la Bellacasa (2017, p. 95) draws out the "affective, ethical and practical" dimensions of caring, and the promise of thinking with the sensorial intensity of touch. In some of the touching exchanges between children, weather and worlds that we have described, we witness a desire for connections, understanding and speculative involvement in the adventure of shaping shared weather worlds (Rooney et al., 2021).

The practice of care is often sidelined or ignored, no doubt due to its historical and ongoing association with the work of women. Along with other feminist thinkers we have drawn on in this book, Puig de la Bellacasa doesn't rally so much against the diminution of the practice of care, but rather draws our attention to care as a necessary, ethical and political practice to make things better. She notes that care:

> goes beyond a moral disposition or wishful thinking to transform how we experience and perceive the things we study. Here care stands for necessary yet mostly dismissed labors of everyday maintenance of life, an ethico-political commitment to neglected things, and the affective remaking of relationships with our objects.
>
> *(2017, p. 66)*

This is important in our relations with weather worlds, and once again is generative when it comes from an action that is repeated or returned to, and where attention is given to relationality and mutuality:

> Care work becomes better when it is done again, creating the specificity of a relation through intensified involvement and knowledge. It requires attention and fine-tuning to the temporal rhythms of an 'other' and to the specific relations that are being woven together.
>
> *(Puig de la Bellacasa, 2015, p. 706)*

The shaping of place with and by weather can be understood as integral to the ways children relate to, return to and learn with, Earth as an act of care (Puig de la Bellacasa, 2017). As we continue to learn with, and to notice children learning with, the rhythms and temporalities of weather worlds, we recognise this as a practice of care, a collective practice that becomes possible when we recognise our mutual vulnerability and connectedness with more-than-human others.

Conclusion

In environmental education, we cannot ignore the crisis of climate change and the destructive impacts that are unfolding across more-than-human weather worlds. Insights from the stories throughout this book have revealed young children's capacity to imagine worlds differently. They have also shown us that this is

Conclusion **147**

not just an act of thinking about what might be, but that doing, making, sensing, caring and weathering with more-than-human others are the actions and relations through which we might recuperate more liveable weather worlds.

The practice of weather learning discussed in this book is a feminist practice. It emphasises the inseparability of humans and weather, and challenges world views that privilege human-centric perspectives. There is no doubt that we need to learn to think and live differently. As we said in the opening of this book, the challenges of climate change will require an approach to learning that helps us to "imagine alternatives" for becoming with the world and to reimagine our place in the world (Common Worlds Research Collective, 2020, p. 2). Understanding our (human) embeddedness within ecologies and weather worlds provides a position from which we can shift our practice from learning *about* weather, to more collective, relational, embodied and situated ways of learning *with* weather.

Weather is familiar. With weather we shape and deepen connections with places, memories and materials, as well as with other creatures, plants and ecologies. The affects of weather stay in our bodies. These sensory, bodily, situated, ordinary relations with weather can open up possibilities for connection to climate and climate change. To shift our thinking towards a feminist weather learning practice is to see ordinary moments, relations and encounters differently, and to (un)learn the ways we see learning with the child at the centre, and instead to attune to child and weather together. We are still learning how to listen better with wind, clouds, rain, land, fire, rocks, dust, critters and trees. We invite you to join us in telling stories, in walking and talking, in noticing the ordinary affects of weather, in making space and time for children to linger with more-than-human companions, in reminding ourselves to think differently, and to weave some threads for flourishing in weather worlds together.

References

Åsberg, C., Thiele, K., & Van der Tuin, I. (2015). Speculative before the turn: Reintroducing feminist materialist performativity. *Cultural Studies Review, 21*(2), 145–172.

Braidotti, R. (2022). *Posthuman feminism*. John Wiley & Sons.

Common Worlds Research Collective. (2020). *Learning to become with the world: Education for future survival*. UNESCO. https://unesdoc.unesco.org/ark:/48223/pf0000374923

Haraway, D. (2013). SF: Science fiction, speculative fabulation, string figures, so far. *Ada: A Journal of Gender, New Media, and Technology, 3*, 1–18. http://dx.doi.org/10.7264/N3KH0K81

Haraway, D. (2016) *Staying with the trouble*. Duke University Press.

Hird, M. J. (2013). Waste, landfills, and an environmental ethic of vulnerability. *Ethics and the Environment, 18*(1), 105–124. https://doi.org/10.2979/ethicsenviro.18.1.105

Neimanis, A., & Walker, R. L. (2014). Weathering: Climate change and the "thick time" of transcorporeality. *Hypatia, 29*(3), 558–575.

Puig de la Bellacasa, M. (2015). Making time for soil: Technoscientific futurity pace of care. *Social Studies of Science, 45*(5), 691–716. https://doi.org/10.1177/0306312715599851

148 Responses: Learning and speculating in a climate change era

Puig de la Bellacasa, M. (2017). *Matters of care: Speculative ethics in more than human worlds.* University of Minnesota Press.

Rooney, T., Blaise, M., & Royds, F. (2021) With shadows, dust and mud: Activating weathering-with pedagogies in early childhood education. *Contemporary Issues in Early Childhood, 22*(2):109–123. https://doi.org/10.1177/1463949120939202

Taylor, A. (2017) Beyond stewardship: Common world pedagogies for the Anthropocene, *Environmental Education Research,* 23(10), 1448–1461. https://doi.org/10.1080/135046 22.2017.1325452

Truman, S. E. (2021). *Feminist speculations and the practice of research-creation: Writing pedagogies and intertextual affects.* Routledge.

Tsing, A. L., (2019) When the things we study respond to each other: Tools for unpacking "the material". In *Anthropos and the material* eds. Harvey, P., Krohn-Hansen, C., & Nustad K.G. Duke University Press, pp. 221–243 (see https://www.dukeupress.edu/anthropos-and-the-material)

INDEX

affect 10, 37, 58, 67, 70–71, 81–92, 95, 103, 118–119, 138, 141, 145–147

air 5, 35, 37, 44, 51, 68–69, 72, 84–91, 98, 105, 107–108, 112, 122, 134; airborne 7, 88, 105, 108; air conditioning 4, 84; *see also* atmosphere

animacy 67, 70

animals 12, 25–29, 41, 52–53, 63, 67–69, 76, 83, 87, 94–97, 104–109, 129–130, 135, 144; dead animals 58, 89, 94–97, 100–105, 108–109, 129–130, 136, 144; *see also* multi-species relations

anthropocentrism *see* human-centrism

art 34, 42, 67, 74, 116

atmosphere 18, 26, 35, 67, 70, 81–92, 95, 108–109

attention 10, 23, 44, 57–60, 85, 89–91, 114, 122, 129, 138, 146; noticing 26, 42, 66–68, 75, 90, 96, 137; paying attention 55, 67, 70, 75, 95–97, 144

attunement 35–38, 53, 59, 82, 92, 119, 122, 138

Barad, Karen 40

Bawaka collective 10, 23, 39, 45–46, 68, 113, 118–119, 122

becoming 16, 21, 42, 44, 46, 118, 124, 147; becoming-with 9–10, 42, 58–59, 71

Berlant, Lauren 71

binary logics 6–7, 16, 21–26, 51, 120, 144

birds 52, 57–58, 82, 86, 91–96, 98–99, 102–103, 108, 136, 140

bodies 8, 10, 26, 42, 44, 53–60, 70, 76, 108, 115–116, 120–122, 143–144; weather bodies 3, 12, 34–40, 81–91, 138; *see also* embodiment

Braidotti, Rosi 39, 55

built environment 38, 41, 50, 84, 103

bush kinders 18–19; *see also* forest schools

bushfire 7, 13, 96, 105–108

care 9, 12, 84, 89–96, 102, 114, 131, 145–147; care of Country 118

Chen, Mel Y 85, 120

child development 8, 16, 19–23, 70, 138; developmentalism 20, 23, 53, 59, 65, 69–70, 67; *see also* postdevelopmentalism

classroom 3, 34, 58, 131–132, 140; beyond the classroom 54, 120; *see also* outdoors, outdoor learning

Clement, Susannah 83

climate change 4–6, 10–12, 23–26, 40, 42, 46, 75, 84, 91–97, 114, 116, 119–123, 134–138, 143–147; climate activists 21; climate science 34, 91, 97; *see also* climate change education

climate change education 17, 20

clothes 6, 35, 44, 49, 58, 72, 81, 84, 87, 104–105, 115, 132

clouds 7, 44, 67, 81, 86, 107–109, 119, 132, 139, 144, 147

collective practice 5, 9–10, 22, 40, 56, 60, 68, 132, 137–138, 147

150 Index

colonial, *see* colonisation
colonisation 11, 23, 41–43, 50, 75–76, 85, 88–89, 138; *see also* decolonisation; postcolonial
common worlds 22, 143
Common Worlds Research Collective 5, 22
COVID 89
creative practice 64, 66–73, 132
curiosity 8, 53, 56, 60, 65, 68, 74, 88, 92, 96, 98–101, 109, 120, 131

Davis, Julie 3, 19
death 12, 25, 42, 64, 68, 74, 87–88, 94–96, 101, 118, 139, 143; *see also* animals; extinction
decolonisation 22, 66, 76
developmentalism *see* child development
Duhn, Iris 38, 109

Earth 9, 12, 17, 34–42, 59, 73, 90–91, 97, 108, 112–123, 131 146; *see also* earth
earth 40, 42, 58–60, 84–85, 89, 95, 108, 123, 112–123, 129; earth science 47; mud 8, 60, 71–73, 98, 112; soil 19, 68, 114, 129–130
ecosystem 9, 89, 95, 97, 99, 108–109, 130, 143
Edensor, Tim 35
education for sustainability 17, 19
Elliott, Sue 20
elements 3, 7, 21, 35, 39, 63, 67–68, 73, 81, 83, 91–92, 100, 108, 114, 122, 135, 138
embodiment 3, 10, 23–26, 34, 54, 71, 81, 90, 138, 143, 147
environmental humanities 15, 23–24, 26, 65
erosion 33, 40, 112
ethics 65, 75, 90–91, 109, 121, 131, 137–138, 145–147
ethnography 5, 20, 26, 49, 64, 70–71, 85
extinction 12, 24, 96–97, 108

feminism 15, 21–26, 64, 81; feminist practice 11, 40, 66, 85, 90, 92, 131, 138, 140–147
fog 113, 117, 120–122
forest schools 18

Gannon, Susanne 84
geological 34, 112, 114–115, 119–120, 124

Haraway, Donna 4, 24–25, 53, 56, 64–65, 67, 90–91, 117–118, 144–145

human-centrism 6, 11, 18, 35, 55, 63, 66, 68, 134, 147; human exceptionalism 6, 144
human-weather relations 4–5, 9, 12, 26, 34, 38, 46, 59, 92, 104, 108, 112, 134

imagine 4, 9–10, 17, 21, 37, 42, 58–59, 82, 98, 107, 116–117, 124, 137–138, 145–147; *see also* speculation
Indigenous perspectives 5, 23, 34, 41–42, 45–46, 66, 68–69, 108, 121, 133–136; notions of Country 41–47, 74–75, 118
Ingold, Tim 10, 34–35, 49, 53, 55, 57, 59
Instone, Lesley 53, 55–56, 68

learning: inquiry learning 133–134; learning environments 49, 71; learning-with 4–5, 9, 34, 53, 56, 59–60, 63, 66, 122–123; weather learning 9, 12, 34, 70, 82–83, 90, 96, 98, 102, 105, 129–132, 135–140, 144–147; *see also* outdoors, outdoor learning; pedagogy
Lee, Nick 16
light 35–37, 57, 59, 67–68, 81, 84, 99, 102, 119, 140
lightning 107, 119
listening 5, 9, 24, 26, 34, 42–46, 53, 66–70, 119, 121, 131, 135–138, 147
living 95–97, 102, 108, 118, 131, 137, 146; and non-living 113, 120–123

MacLeavy, Julie 23
Massey, Doreen 39, 113, 116–118
materiality 10, 18, 22, 26, 33, 38–40, 58, 76, 81–85, 90, 108, 112, 116, 129, 134, 144, 147; *see also* new materialism
meteorological 34, 47, 122, 132
Millei, Zsuzsa 83
more-than-human 6, 8–11, 13, 15, 17, 22–25, 34, 38–40, 45–58, 64–65, 68, 70, 81–82, 89–90, 95–96, 109, 116, 119, 131, 137, 144–147; non-human 3, 6, 10, 15, 26, 40, 55–56, 59, 65–69, 76, 114
movement 16–18, 36–39, 53–55, 59–60, 66–71, 74, 76, 94, 102, 113, 122
multi-species relations 9–12, 22, 94–109, 131, 141, 143

naturecultures 22, 24
Neimanis, Astrida 10, 35, 37, 40, 46, 116
new materialism 6, 23
Nxumalo, Fikile 6, 22, 65, 76, 95

Index 151

outdoors 5–8, 16, 20, 60, 75, 133; outdoor learning 17–19, 135

Pacini-Ketchabaw, Veronica 6, 22, 40, 76, 96
pedagogy 5, 9–12, 17–19, 21–23, 47, 49, 52–54, 67, 77, 83, 96, 109, 113, 123, 130, 132, 137–140, 143–145
place 10, 15–16, 23, 26, 33, 36, 41, 43–46, 50–60, 63, 69–76, 109, 113–123, 135, 141; place-making 12, 34, 38–39, 146
plants 12, 37, 52, 63, 69, 91, 94–95, 103–109, 114, 129–130, 135; see also multi-species relations
Plumwood, Val 6, 25
pollution 7, 52, 68, 84, 89, 117, 120–121
postcolonial 22–23; see also colonisation; decolonisation
postdevelopmentalism 15, 20–23, 26, 59, 138
poststructuralism 23
Povinelli, Elizabeth 26, 113, 117–123
Prout, Alan 16
Puig de la Bellacasa, María 90–91, 144–146

rain 4, 7, 33–34, 42–44, 69, 73, 76, 82–91, 94–95, 105–108, 112–113, 136–140; storm 13, 55, 40, 82, 95, 107, 143
Rautio, Pauliina 6, 11, 47, 54
rocks 20, 39, 50–51, 53, 57, 68, 81, 113–117, 130; fossils 112
Rose, Deborah Bird 6–7, 25, 64, 71, 97, 102, 118, 135–136

science 19–20, 25, 34, 47, 97, 114, 132–134
seasons 8, 34, 39–40, 51, 69, 81, 104, 106, 131–136, 141
sensory 3, 8, 10, 18, 35, 37, 49, 53–56, 63, 69, 82–86, 89–92, 102, 104, 124, 133, 138; senses 73, 84, 122, 133
shadows 36, 57, 59, 81, 98–99, 102, 109; see also light
singing 41, 44, 47, 73–77, 86, 90–91, 132, 134
snow 7, 34, 59, 82–83, 119, 132
Solnit, Rebecca 56
Somerville, Margaret 6, 19, 64
song see singing
space 12, 15–19, 39, 55, 60, 84, 89, 97, 108–109, 117–122, 143; Space 120

speculation 9–10, 21, 26, 34, 54, 71, 131, 138, 141, 144–146
Stengers, Isabelle 25, 53, 59, 75
Stewart, Kathleen 71, 84–85
stones see rocks
story 44, 63–65, 67, 70–74, 100–101, 106, 115, 132
sunshine 7, 34, 38, 83, 95, 102, 104, 107–108, 138, 140, 143
sustainability 17, 19, 134

Taguchi, Hillevi Lenz 6, 22
Taylor, Affrica 5–6, 16, 21–22, 40, 49, 68, 76, 89
technology 6, 16, 25, 84; weather apps 33, 63, 107
temperature 39, 59, 84, 98, 116, 135
temporality 23, 26, 71, 96, 116–119, 123, 134, 146
time 5, 12, 34–37, 41, 53–55, 63, 100, 112–120, 136, 138–140; non-linear time 74, 89; slowing down 8, 25, 53, 56, 67
transcorporeality 37, 87, 105
Tsing, Anna 9–10, 25–26, 96, 137

uncertainty 4–8, 10–11, 23, 39, 53, 60, 65, 96, 101, 105, 117, 131, 135, 137, 140

van Dooren, Thom 26, 96–97, 102, 116, 119
Vannini, Phillip 10, 38–39, 83
vulnerability 5, 12, 39–40, 73, 94–101, 131, 143–146

Walker, Rachel 10, 35, 37, 40, 46, 116
walking 11–12, 24, 34, 36, 44, 49–60, 66–71, 97, 118, 122, 129–131, 138, 141; wayfaring 55, 60; wayfinding 60, 129
water 3, 5, 38–51, 57–58, 72–75, 81–88, 91, 98–100, 114–115, 136, 139–140; see also rain
weather worlds 8–12, 34–37, 40, 42, 46, 53, 59–60, 63, 66–73, 76, 82–90, 104, 109, 119–120, 131–147
wind 23, 33, 44–45, 51, 59, 67–70, 81, 88–89, 102, 107, 120, 136, 147
worlding 40, 56, 60, 76, 144–145
Wright, Sarah 41–42

Yusoff, Kathryn 26, 113–114, 120

Printed in the United States
by Baker & Taylor Publisher Services